MATHEMATICS

R.N. ROWE B.Sc. M.Sc. F.I.S. F.I.M.A.

Dean of Faculty of Management and Policy Studies

South Bank Polytechnic

DP Publications
Aldine Place
142/144 Uxbridge Road
London W12 8AW
1991

D0996038

Acknowledgements

I would like to express my than[...]
Department of Business and Finance[...]
Russell, for their assistance in the [...]
Celine, for her helpful suggestions a[...]

A CIP catalogue record for this book i[...]

First edition1991

ISBN 1 870941 78 0

Copyright © R.N.Rowe 1991

Typeset by:
KAI Typesetting and Design
21 Sycamore Rise, Nottingham

Printed by:
The Guernsey Press Co. Ltd.
Vale, Guernsey

Contents

Preface

General

Aim

The aim of this book is to provide a course text for the many courses that introduce business mathematics and statistics, quantitative methods, etc to students who do not need to be, and very often aren't, particularly mathematically minded.

The courses that this text is intended for include Business Studies degree and diploma courses as well as the whole range of other business related courses and those courses containing a business component - such courses will usually have an entry requirement equivalent to GCSE / 'O' level in mathematics (or a related subject).

The book is intended as a first course and it assumes a knowledge equivalent to that covered by *A Refresher in Basic Mathematics* by the same author.

Need

It is the author's experience that students on the type of courses mentioned require an easy-to-read textbook with the emphasis on worked examples supplemented by exercises with answers - all at an introductory level. Such a book differs from the many textbooks which go to great depth and are not always suitable for those students who require an introductory first course.

Approach

The book is divided into two parts - **Business Mathematics** and **Statistics**. Each topic has an introduction/outline followed by a series of worked examples to illustrate the technique in question. The concepts and methods are presented in a clear and concise manner that provides a foundation for further, more detailed study. As well as being used as a text in its own right, the book's emphasis on worked examples enables it to also be used to supplement a textbook that covers the subject areas to a greater depth.

Introduction

Many management decisions are based on a variety of types of information including very little or incomplete information. Various methods involving mathematical and statistical techniques have been formulated that help the manager to analyse, organise and evaluate information for use in business decision making. *A First Course in Business Mathematics and Statistics* looks firstly at the mathematical and then the statistical areas of the subject that underpin many of the more advanced business applications.

Part 1
Business Mathematics

Introduction

This part consists of four chapters - the first two dealing with mathematical techniques needed for financial calculations and the latter two dealing with matrix applications that introduce mathematical concepts which underpin management decisions relating to the use of resources. In each case the first of the two chapters introduces the techniques, and the second demonstrates applications.

The financial mathematics element is relevant to situations in everyday life as well as to business applications. It forms the basis of more advanced techniques which facilitate decision making at all levels eg comparison of different types of mortgage/loan available; comparison of returns on investments, etc. The matrix applications element, including the formulation and solution of equations representing practical situations, form a basis for more sophisticated business applications in Operational Research including Linear Programming and Modelling.

1 Sequences and Series

1. Introduction

Sequences and Series have a wide range of applications in a variety of areas. In particular two types of series, Arithmetic Progressions and Geometric Progressions, form the basis of some fundamental financial calculations, which you will come to in Chapter 2. In this chapter the basic concepts of Sequences and Series are introduced and these are developed to consider Arithmetic Progressions and Geometric Progressions.

2. Sequences

A sequence is a set of ordered values which progress from term to term in a fixed pattern.

Examples

i)   4, 9, 14, 19, ...

ii) 3, 6, 12, 24, ...

iii) 1, 4, 9, 16, ...

3. Series

A series is the sum of the terms of a sequence.

Examples

i)   4 + 9 + 14 + 19 + ...

ii) 3 + 6 + 12 + 24 + ...

iii) 1 + 4 + 9 + 16 + ...

In sections 4 and 5, two particularly useful types of series will be considered, namely Arithmetic Progressions and Geometric Progressions. These two types of series form the basis of some important financial calculations.

4. Arithmetic progressions

A series is said to be an 'Arithmetic Progression' if it has the following form:

$$S = a + [a + d] + [a + 2d] + [a + 3d] + ... + [a + (n - 1)d]$$

where   a = first term of the series.

d = common difference.

n = number of terms.

Examples

i) $S = 4 + 9 + 14 + 19 + 24 + 29$;

   $a = 4$; $d = 5$; $n = 6$;

ii) $S = 1 + 2^{1}/_{2} + 4 + 5^{1}/_{2}$;

   $a = 1$; $d = 1^{1}/_{2}$; $n = 4$

iii) $S = 30 + 27 + 24 + 21 + 18$;

   $a = 30$; $d = -3$; $n = 5$

4.1 n^{th} term of an Arithmetic Progression

This is given by:

$$n^{th} \text{ term} = a + (n-1)d$$

Example

$S = 1 + 4 + 7 + 10 + 13 + \ldots$

   $(\therefore a = 1; \ d = 3;)$

   $7^{th} \text{ term} = a + 6d = 1 + 18 = \mathbf{19}$;

   $10^{th} \text{ term} = a + 9d = 1 + 27 = \mathbf{28}$

4.2 Sum of an Arithmetic Progression

The sum of the first n terms of an Arithmetic Progression is given by

$$S = \frac{n}{2}[2a + (n-1)d]$$

Example

$S = 1 + 3 + 5 + 7 + \ldots$

Find the sum of the first 12 terms of this Arithmetic Progression.

   $n = 12$; $a = 1$; $d = 2$;

   $S = \frac{12}{2}[2 + 11(2)] = 6[2 + 22] = \mathbf{144}$

5. Geometric progressions

A series is said to be a 'Geometric Progression' if it has the following form:

   $S = a + ar + ar^2 + ar^3 + \ldots + ar^{n-1}$

where a = first term of the series

   r = common ratio

   n = number of terms

Examples

i) $S = 3 + 6 + 12 + 24 + 48$

   $a = 3;\ \ r = 2;\ \ n = 5;$

ii) $S = 1 + \frac{1}{2} + \frac{1}{4} + \frac{1}{8} + \frac{1}{16} + \frac{1}{32};$

   $a = 1;\ \ r = \frac{1}{2};\ \ n = 6$

iii) $S = 1 - 2 + 4 - 8 + 16 - 32 + 64;$

   $a = 1;\ \ r = -2;\ \ n = 7$

5.1 n^{th} term of a Geometric Progression

This is given by:

$$n^{th} \text{ term} = ar^{n-1}$$

Example

$S = 1 + 2 + 4 + 8 + 16 + \ldots\ldots$

   $(\therefore a = 1;\ \ r = 2;)$

   $7^{th} \text{ term} = ar^6 = 1 \times 2^6 = \mathbf{64};$

   $10^{th} \text{ term} = ar^9 = 1 \times 2^9 = \mathbf{512}$

5.2 Sum of a Geometric Progression

The sum of the first n terms of a Geometric Progression is given by

$$S = \frac{a(r^n - 1)}{r - 1} = \frac{a(1 - r^n)}{1 - r}$$

Example

$S = 1 + 3 + 9 + 27 + 81 + \ldots\ldots\ldots$

Find the sum of the first 7 terms of this Geometric Progression.

   $n = 7;\ a = 1;\ \ r = 3;$

   $S = \dfrac{1(3^7 - 1)}{3 - 1} = \mathbf{1093}$

 Exercises (Answers on page 7)

1. Determine which of the following series are in arithmetic progression. In the case of an Arithmetic Progression write down the next three terms.

   a) $3 + 6 + 9 + 12 + 15 + 18 \ldots..$

   b) $25 + 19 + 13 + 7 + 1 - 5 \ldots..$

   c) $5 + 10 + 14 + 20 + 25 \ldots.$

   d) $(3a - 2b) + (4a - b) + (5a) + (6a + b) \ldots.$

2. Determine which of the following series are in geometric progression. In the case of a Geometric Progression write down the next three terms.

   a) $4 + 8 + 16 + 32 + 64$ ....

   b) $1 + \frac{1}{4} + \frac{1}{16} + \frac{1}{48}$ ......

   c) $12 - 4 + \frac{4}{3} - \frac{4}{9}$ ......

3. Find the 18th term and the sum of the first 18 terms of the following progression.

   $$2 + 6 + 10 + 14 ....$$

4. Find the 7th term and the sum of the first 7 terms of the following progression

   $$12 + 16 + \frac{64}{3} ....$$

5. Find the 12th term and the sum of the first 15 terms of the following progression

   $$8 + \frac{19}{3} + \frac{14}{3} ......$$

6. Find the last term and the sum of each of the following series

   a) $2\frac{1}{2} + 6 + 9\frac{1}{2}$ ..... (16 terms)

   b) $36 + 29 + 22 +$ ..... (21 terms)

   c) $9 - 4\frac{1}{2} + 2\frac{1}{4}$ ..... (10 terms)

7. Find the 10th term, the sum of the first 10 terms, and the sum of the first 13 terms of the following series

   $$(2x + 3y) + (x + y) - (y) ....$$

8. Find the value of K such that the following series are geometric progressions and hence find the next 3 terms

   a) $(2K - 5) + (K - 4) + (10 - 3K)$ ....

   b) $(K + 1) + (K + 2) + (K + 5)$ ......

9. The sum of the first n terms of an Arithmetic Progression is given by

   $$S_n = \frac{n}{2} [2a + (n - 1)d]$$

   Derive this formula

10. The sum of the first n terms of a Geometric Progression is given by:

    $$S_n = \frac{a(r^n - 1)}{r - 1} = \frac{a(1 - r^n)}{1 - r}$$

    Derive this formula

Short Answers

1. a) $21 + 24 + 27$
    b) $-11 - 17 - 23$
    c) *not A.P.*
    d) $(7a + 2b) + (8a + 3b) + (9a + 4b)$

2. a) $128 + 256 + 512$
    b) *not G.P.*
    c) $4/27 - 4/81 + 4/243$

3. $70; \ 648$

4. $67.42; \ 233.695$

5. $-31/3; \ -55$

6. a) $55; \ 460$
    b) $-104; \ -714$
    c) $-0.0176; \ 5.994$

7. $-(7x + 15y); \ -5(5x + 12y); \ -13(4x + 9y)$

8. a) 3 or $22/7$;
    $-1 + 1 - 1$ (when $K = 3$)
    $-8/21 + 16/63 - 32/189$ (when $K = 22/7$)

    b) $-1/2$;
    next 3 terms: $27/2 + 81/2 + 243/2$

9. Proof

10. Proof

2 Financial Mathematics

1. Introduction

Financial mathematics forms the basis of many aspects of everyday life and, in particular, calculations of interest on mortgages and other types of loans, investments etc which affect a great number of people and businesses. A whole range of financial calculations such as these are, in fact, applications of Geometric and Arithmetic progressions (covered in Chapter 1).

In this Chapter, following a brief revision of percentage calculations, financial applications of arithmetic and geometric progressions, including interest calculations, are considered. These applications are then developed further by considering more complex situations.

2. Percentages

Examples

i)   15% of 60 = 60(0.15) = 9

ii)   8% of 125 = 125(0.08) = 10

iii) 7^1/$_2$% of 78 = 78(0.075) = 5.85

iv) Increase 60 by 15%

$$= 60 + 60(0.15)$$

$$= 60(1 + 0.15)$$

$$= 60(1.15) = 69$$

v)   Increase 125 by 8%

$$= 125(1 + 0.08)$$

$$= 125(1.08)$$

$$= 135$$

vi) Decrease 125 by 8%

$$= 125(1 - 0.08)$$

$$= 125(0.92)$$

$$= 115$$

3. Applications of arithmetic progressions

Examples

i)   Consider an official who has been working in local government for the past 10 years. His starting salary was £7156 with annual increments of £250. Calculate his present salary per annum, and also the *total* amount he has earned over the ten year period.

This example can be treated as an example of an arithmetic progression as the annual increment is a fixed amount.

The nth term of an A.P. $= a + (n - 1)d$

Salary during first year	= 1st term	= a	= £7156
Salary during second year	= 2nd term	= a + d	= £7156 + £250
...	...	...	
...	...	...	
...	...	...	
His present salary	= 10th term	= a + 9d	

$$= 7156 + 9(250)$$
$$= 7156 + 2250$$
$$= £9406$$

The sum of the first n terms of an A.P. is given by

$$S_n = \frac{n}{2}[2a + (n - 1)d]$$

The total amount he has earned over 10 years is given by

$$S_n = \frac{10}{2}[2(7156) + 9(250)]$$
$$= 5[14312 + 2250]$$
$$= 5(16562)$$
$$= £82810$$

ii)   A machine is bought for £8250 and depreciation is assessed as £750 per year. What will be its book value at the end of 8 years.

NB Remember depreciation is a negative increment

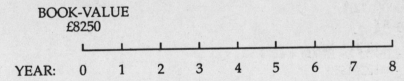

BOOK-VALUE
£8250

YEAR: 0   1   2   3   4   5   6   7   8

Book value at end of 8 years $= a + 8d$
$$= 8250 + 8(-750)$$
$$= 8250 - 8(750)$$
$$= £2250$$

iii)   A person invests their total savings of £2000 at 7% p.a. At the end of each year the interest is sent to the person who keeps it on one side (not in an account) in case of an emergency. Assuming no emergency occurs, how much will the person's savings (including interest) be worth at the end of 8 years?

7% of £2000 = £140

After 8 years the total savings (including interest) will be worth

£2000 + 8(£140) = £2000 + £1120

$\qquad$ = £3120

(This is an example of simple interest)

4. Compound interest

A very important application of Geometric Progressions comes into play when money is invested with compound interest. In this case the interest is a stated percentage of the amount invested and is not paid out to the investor but is added to the amount invested. This interest thereafter also earns interest, and the interest is said to be compounded or converted into 'principal', this latter term being applied generally to money that earns interest. Compound interest contrasts with 'Simple Interest' where the interest itself is not added to the 'principal' in that it does not, itself, subsequently earn interest.

NB Unless stated otherwise, interest is generally assumed to be compounded.

A general formula for compound interest is given by

$$A = P(1 + i)^n$$

where $\quad$ n = number of periods

$\qquad$ i = interest rate (expressed as a decimal)

$\qquad$ P = Principal

$\qquad$ A = Accumulated amount

Examples

i) $\quad$ If £1000 is invested for 4 years at 12% per annum compound interest, how much interest is paid?

$$A = P(1 + i)^n$$

$$= 1000 (1 + 0.12)^4$$

$$= 1000(1.12)^4$$

$$= £1573.52$$

Interest paid = £1573.52 − £1000 = **£573.52**

ii) $\quad$ If £500 is required in 5 years time, and the annual rate of interest is 8%, how much must be invested now?

Unless stated otherwise, interest is generally assumed to be compounded.

$$A = P(1 + i)^n$$

$$500 = P(1 + 0.08)^5$$

$$P = \frac{500}{(1.08)^5} = \frac{500}{1.4693}$$

P = £340.29

NB This is an example of 'present value' – see section 7.

iii) £5000 is required in 5 years time. If £3000 is available for investment now, at what annual rate of interest must it be invested?

$$A = P(1 + i)^n$$

$$5000 = 3000 (1 + i)^5$$

$$(1 + i)^5 = {}^5/_3$$

$$1 + i = \sqrt[5]{{}^5/_3} = 1.107$$

$$i = 0.107$$

Interest rate = **10.7%**

iv) If £1800 is invested at 8% p.a., compounded semi–annually, how much will have accumulated after 5 years?

Here we are dealing with periods of 'half a year' and hence n = 10 and i = 0.4

$$A = P(1 + i)^n$$

$$= 1800(1 + 0.04)^{10}$$

$$= £2664.44$$

NB If interest had been compounded quarterly in this example, then we would have:

n = 20 (there are 20 'quarters' in a five year period)

and

i = 0.2 (ie 2% per quarter)

5. Depreciation

Depreciation by a fixed percentage over a period of time can be considered as an extension of the compound interest formula with a negative value of i.

Example

A machine cost £4800 new. If it depreciates at a rate of 30%p.a., how much will it be worth after 10 years?

Value of machine after 10 years = $4800(1 - 0.3)^{10}$ = **£135.59**

6. Regular equal payments

Consider the following example:

i) A person invests £100 at the start of each year for 30 years. If the rate of interest is 10% p.a. how much will their savings be worth at the end of this time?

This situation can be represented by the diagram on the following page with time period 0 representing now, time period 1 representing one years time, time period 2 representing two years time, etc.

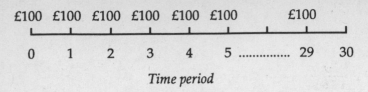

Amount invested

Time period

After 30 years the savings are worth:

$$S = 100(1.1)^{30} + 100(1.1)^{29} + 100(1.1)^{28} + ... + 100(1.1)^2 + 100(1.1)$$

$$S = 100(1.1) + 100(1.1)^2 + ... + 100(1.1)^{30}$$

This is a G.P. with $a = 100(1.1)$; $r = 1.1$; $n = 30$

$$S = \frac{a(r^n - 1)}{r - 1} = \frac{100(1.1)[(1.1)^{30} - 1]}{1.1 - 1} = £18,095$$

ii) **Exercise**

In the previous worked example, how much would the person's savings be worth if the £100 had been invested at the *end* of each year?

Answer: £16450

Exercise

Repeat the previous worked example, ie. 6 i), assuming interest is compounded semi–annually.

Answer: £19015.90

7. Present value

The concept of 'present value' provides a means of comparing alternative loans or investments and is fundamental to business decision making. This section introduces the basics of 'present value' and the importance of the timing of payments.

An amount of money that is to be received or paid out at a future date has a *present value*. For example, if an amount of say £300 is to be received in 2 years time, the 'present value' of this amount is what it is worth now, at the present time – this will be less than £300. This can be seen by considering, alternatively, that if we were to receive £300 now, it could be invested and would clearly be worth more in 2 years time. The 'present value' of £300 that is to be received in 2 years time is, in fact, the amount that we would have to invest now, at a given rate of interest, that would accumulate to £300 in 2 years.

To calculate the present value of an amount, we can rearrange the compound interest formula as follows:

$$A = P(1 + i)^n$$

$$P = \frac{A}{(1 + i)^n}$$

Examples

i) Calculate the present value of £300, to be received in two years time, assuming an interest rate of 8%.

$$P = \frac{A}{(1 + i)^n}$$

$$P = \frac{300}{(1 + 0.08)^2} = \frac{300}{1.1664}$$

$$= £257.20$$

Hence the present value equals **£257.20**

This concept can be extended to cover a range of payments over time as illustrated in the following examples.

ii) Calculate the present value of receiving £100 in one years time, £250 in two years time and £500 in three years time assuming an interest rate of 10% p.a.?

$$P = \frac{100}{(1 + 0.1)} + \frac{250}{(1 + 0.1)^2} + \frac{500}{(1 + 0.1)^3}$$

$$= £673.18$$

Hence the present value equals **£673.18**

iii) Calculate the present value of receiving an annuity of £400 a year for 20 years, assuming an interest rate of 10%.

Assuming that the annuity is received at the end of each year, this situation can be represented by the following diagram

Amount received

Time period

$$P = \frac{400}{(1 + 0.1)} + \frac{400}{(1 + 0.1)^2} + \cdots + \frac{400}{(1 + 0.1)^{20}}$$

This is a Geometric Progression with:

$$a = \frac{400}{(1 + 0.1)}; \quad r = \frac{1}{(1 + 0.1)}; \quad n = 20$$

Using the formula for the sum of a Geometric Progression we have:

$$P = \frac{a(1 - r^n)}{1 - r} = \frac{\frac{400}{1.1}\left(1 - \frac{1}{1.1^{20}}\right)}{\left(1 - \frac{1}{1.1}\right)} = £3405.43$$

Exercises *(Answers on page 17)*

1. £700 is invested at 5% per annum compound interest. What will the account be worth after 20 years?

2. If £7500 is required in 10 years time, how much should be invested now assuming an interest rate of 10% p.a.?

3. A machine costs £6200 and is expected to last for 14 years and then have a scrap value of £740. If depreciation is to be assessed as a fixed amount each year, what should this amount be?

   If the machine is to be depreciated at a fixed percentage of the current book value, what should this percentage be?

4. The salary of a certain part–time company secretary is increased by a fixed increment each year. If his total earnings over nine years are £23,400 and his salary in the final year is £2950, what was his salary in the sixth year?

5. If £600 is invested in an account at 8% p.a., how much will the account be worth after 6 years if interest is added

   a) annually,

   b) semi–annually,

   c) quarterly?

6. A company sets aside £5000 each year out of profits to form a reserve fund, which is invested at 6% per annum compound interest. What will be the value of the fund after 10 years?

7. A family invests £50 at the beginning of each year, and compound interest is added at $5\frac{1}{2}\%$ per annum. How much will they have accumulated after 15 years?

8. At the end of each year £200 is invested at 7% p.a.. How much will have been saved at the end of 5 years?

9. a) How much do I need to invest now at $8\frac{1}{2}\%$ p.a. to have £400 in two years time?

   b) £700 is required in three years time. If £500 is available for investment now, at what rate must it be invested?

   c) £350 is invested in a fund each year. How much is the fund worth at the end of seven years, assuming an interest rate of 8% p.a., if the money is invested:

   i) At the end of each year.

   ii) At the beginning of each year.

10. Each year a company invests £500 out of its profits into a special fund. Interest is added at a rate of $7\frac{1}{2}\%$ p.a.. At the end of six years the fund is closed. At this point £700 is withdrawn from the fund and the remainder is invested at a rate of 8% p.a. for three years (interest is now to be added semi–annually). How much is the fund worth at the end of this period?

11. A company buys a machine for £5000 at the beginning of the year. Maintenance is to be carried out on the machine at the end of each year. The first maintenance costs £130 (£100 for labour costs, and £30 for materials), and at each subsequent maintenance, labour costs are expected to increase by 10% (over the labour cost of the previous maintenance) and material costs are expected to increase by £5 (over the material cost of the previous maintenance).

At the end of twelve years the machine is sold for £300 as scrap.

Calculate the total cost of the machine (including maintenance costs) to the company.

State any assumptions that you make.

12. a) A firm buys a machine for £10,000. The machine depreciates by £850 in the first year, by £800 in the second year, by 9% (of its current value) in both the third and the fourth years, and by $7\frac{1}{2}$% per year thereafter.

How much will the machine be worth at the end of the eleventh year?

b) A company decides to invest £1000 at the end of each year at a rate of 12% per year.

How much will the fund be worth at the end of seven years?

c) A firm decides that it will need £12,000 in 4 years time to purchase some new equipment. In order to meet this cost, the firm decides to invest an equal amount at the end of each year at a rate of 14% per year.

How much should this amount be?

13. a) On 1 Jan 1986 a firm bought a machine at a cost of £50,000. Depreciation at the end of each year is calculated at the rate of 20 per cent of the machine's value at the beginning of the year. What would be the value of the machine on 1 Jan. 1991?

b) On 1 Jan 1995 the firm intends to buy a replacement machine which is expected to cost £75,000; at the same time the old machine will be traded–in in part exchange at its depreciated value (assuming same depreciation rate as in part (a) of question). If the firm can obtain interest of 15 per cent p.a., compounded semi–annually, on money invested, what amount should it invest on 1 Jan. 1986 to meet the cost of the replacement machine?

c) Based on your knowledge of economics and finance, discuss briefly any considerations which might be relevant to a firm in a 'real life' situation such as the above.

14. a) Explain, by use of examples, the difference between an arithmetic progression and a geometric progression.

b) For each of the following series, find the 13th term and also the sum to 13 terms.

   i) $2 - 4 + 8 \ldots$

   ii) $12 + 7 + 2 \ldots$

   iii) $\frac{3}{2} + \frac{15}{8} + \frac{75}{32} \ldots$

c) A Company buys five cars for £6000 each. Each car is expected to last for 10 years and then to be sold for £200 as scrap.

The cars require servicing every six months and the cost of servicing is divided into two parts viz. labour costs and material costs.

The labour cost is set at £30 per car for the first service, while for each subsequent service the cost will increase by 7% on the previous service labour cost.

The cost of materials required for servicing each car is expected to be £25 for the first service and this amount will increase by £5 at each subsequent service.

Calculate the total cost of the five cars to the company.

15. a) The pattern of sales of a new product in £ 00's per month for the first five months is represented by the sequence:–

    63.00, 67.41, 72.13, 77.18, 82.58

    If this sales pattern continues, estimate the sales for the 12th month and the total sales for the first year.

    b) Arthur Clarke, a part–time employee, earned £3000 for the year ending 31st December, 1980. In following years this amount increased by 8% each year. Arthur also qualified for a fixed London weighting Allowance of £350.00 per annum.

    i) What will Arthur's salary be for the year ending 31st December 1989?

    ii) What will be his total salary from 1st January, 1980 to 31st December, 1989?

16. Calculate the present value of receiving £850 in three years time assuming an interest rate of 9% per annum.

17. Calculate the present value of an annuity of £750 a year for 15 years assuming an interest rate of 8% per annum.

Short answers

1. £1857 approx
2. £2891.57
3. a) £390 p.a.
   b) 14.1%
4. £2687.50
5. a) £952.12
   b) £960.62
   c) £965.06
6. £65,904
7. £1,182
8. £1150.15
9. a) £339.78
   b) 11.869%
   c) i) £3122.98
      ii) £3372.82
10. £3697.27

11. £7158.12
12. a) £4006.46
    b) £10,089
    c) £2438.46
13. a) £16,384
    b) £18,578
    c) Discussion
14. a) Discussion
    b) i) 8192, 5462
       ii) − 48, −234
       iii) 21.827872, 103.13936
    c) £41256.84
15. a) £13261, £112698
    b) £6347.03, £46959.87
16. £656.36
17. £6419.61 (assuming paid at end of year)

3 | Matrices

1. Introduction

Matrices have a wide range of applications and are used in many advanced quantitative techniques. Matrices can be used to present data in tabular form but some of their most important applications are in the areas of operational research and statistics. In this chapter the basics of matrix algebra are explained and these concepts are developed further in Chapter 4.

2. Definition

A matrix is a rectangular array of numbers (referred to as elements) arranged into rows and columns. It is customary to enclose a matrix in either curved or square brackets, and to denote matrices by capital letters (lower case letters are used to denote the elements of a matrix).

Example

$$A = \begin{pmatrix} a & b \\ c & d \end{pmatrix} \text{ or } A = \begin{bmatrix} a & b \\ c & d \end{bmatrix}$$

A matrix is said to be of order m x n if it has m rows and n columns.

Example

$$A = \begin{bmatrix} 1 & 0 & -2 \\ 3 & 1 & 4 \end{bmatrix}$$

The order of A is 2 x 3

If a matrix has only one row, it is referred to as a *row vector*.

If a matrix has only one column it is referred to as a *column vector*.

If the number of rows equals the number of columns the matrix is said to be *square*.

3. Determinants

The determinant of a matrix is defined as the number obtained from the elements of the matrix by specified operations (determinants are defined for square matrices only)

The specified operations and the customary notation are given below:

i)   Consider a 2 × 2 matrix given by

$$A = \begin{bmatrix} a & b \\ c & d \end{bmatrix}$$

The determinant of A is given by

$$|A| = \begin{vmatrix} a & b \\ c & d \end{vmatrix} = ad - bc$$

Example

If $A = \begin{bmatrix} 2 & 1 \\ 4 & 3 \end{bmatrix}$

then

$|A| = (2 \times 3) - (1 \times 4) = 6 - 4 = 2$

Therefore $|A| = 2$

ii) Consider a 3×3 matrix given by

$B = \begin{bmatrix} a & b & c \\ d & e & f \\ g & h & i \end{bmatrix}$

The determinant of B is given by

$|B| = a\begin{vmatrix} e & f \\ h & i \end{vmatrix} - b\begin{vmatrix} d & f \\ g & i \end{vmatrix} + c\begin{vmatrix} d & e \\ g & h \end{vmatrix}$

Example

$B = \begin{bmatrix} 1 & 2 & 1 \\ 0 & 1 & 2 \\ 1 & 0 & 3 \end{bmatrix}$

then

$|B| = 1\begin{vmatrix} 1 & 2 \\ 0 & 3 \end{vmatrix} - 2\begin{vmatrix} 0 & 2 \\ 1 & 3 \end{vmatrix} + 1\begin{vmatrix} 0 & 1 \\ 1 & 0 \end{vmatrix}$

$= 1(3 - 0) - 2(0 - 2) + 1(0 - 1)$

$= 3 + 4 - 1 = 6$

Hence $|B| = 6$

4. Addition and subtraction of matrices

In order to be able to add (or subtract) matrices, the matrices concerned must be of the same order. The process of addition (or subtraction) involves adding (or subtracting) the corresponding elements of the matrices concerned.

Example

$A = \begin{bmatrix} 2 & 1 & 1 \\ 0 & 3 & 2 \end{bmatrix} \quad B = \begin{bmatrix} 1 & 0 & 1 \\ 2 & 2 & 1 \end{bmatrix}$

$A + B = \begin{bmatrix} 3 & 1 & 2 \\ 2 & 5 & 3 \end{bmatrix} \quad A - B = \begin{bmatrix} 1 & 1 & 0 \\ -2 & 1 & 1 \end{bmatrix}$

Example

Three customers enter an off-licence. Customer 1 buys 3 bottles of wine, 1 bottle of whisky and 1 bottle of brandy; Customer 2 buys 1 bottle of wine and 2 bottles of whisky and Customer 3 buys 1 bottle of whisky and 3 bottles of brandy. Express each customer's order as a matrix (i.e. a row vector) and hence, by means of matrix addition, obtain a matrix giving the total order for the 3 customers. (The relevant matrices are shown on the following page)

	Wine	Whisky	Brandy
Customer 1	3	1	1
Customer 2	1	2	0
Customer 3	0	1	3
Total order	4	4	4

5. Multiplication of a matrix by a constant

Multiplication of a matrix by a constant involves multiplying each element of the matrix by the constant.

Example

$$A = \begin{bmatrix} 3 & 2 \\ -1 & 0 \\ 2 & 1 \end{bmatrix}; \quad 3A = 3 \begin{bmatrix} 3 & 2 \\ -1 & 0 \\ 2 & 1 \end{bmatrix} = \begin{bmatrix} 9 & 6 \\ -3 & 0 \\ 6 & 3 \end{bmatrix}$$

6. Matrix multiplication

Consider two matrices A (of order m × n) and B (of order p × q). The product of A and B (written AB) can be calculated if and only if n = p. The order of AB is then m × q.

If n ≠ p (ie n is not equal to p) then the product AB is not defined. Further, it should be noted that generally AB ≠ BA.

The elements of AB are calculated as follows:

The element in the ith row and j^{th} column of AB is the product of the ith row vector of A and the jth column vector of B.

Example

$$A = \begin{bmatrix} 2 & 1 \\ 0 & 2 \end{bmatrix} \quad B = \begin{bmatrix} 3 & 1 & 1 \\ 1 & 0 & 2 \end{bmatrix} \quad C = \begin{bmatrix} 1 & 0 \\ 2 & 1 \\ 3 & 2 \end{bmatrix}$$

i) $AB = \begin{bmatrix} 2 & 1 \\ 0 & 2 \end{bmatrix} \times \begin{bmatrix} 3 & 1 & 1 \\ 1 & 0 & 2 \end{bmatrix} = \begin{bmatrix} 2.3 + 1.1 & 2.1 + 1.0 & 2.1 + 1.2 \\ 0.3 + 2.1 & 0.1 + 2.0 & 0.1 + 2.2 \end{bmatrix} = \begin{bmatrix} 7 & 2 & 4 \\ 2 & 0 & 4 \end{bmatrix}$

[Order: (2 × 2) (2 × 3)]   *[Order: (2 × 3)]*

ii) $BA = \begin{bmatrix} 3 & 1 & 1 \\ 1 & 0 & 2 \end{bmatrix} \times \begin{bmatrix} 2 & 1 \\ 0 & 2 \end{bmatrix}$ Multiplication not possible

[Order: (2 × 3) (2 × 2)]

iii) $CA = \begin{bmatrix} 1 & 0 \\ 2 & 1 \\ 3 & 2 \end{bmatrix} \times \begin{bmatrix} 2 & 1 \\ 0 & 2 \end{bmatrix} = \begin{bmatrix} 1.2 + 0.0 & 1.1 + 0.2 \\ 2.2 + 1.0 & 2.1 + 1.2 \\ 3.2 + 2.0 & 3.1 + 2.2 \end{bmatrix} = \begin{bmatrix} 2 & 1 \\ 4 & 4 \\ 6 & 7 \end{bmatrix}$

[Order: (3 × 2) (2 × 2)]   *[Order: (3 × 2)]*

Example

A customer visits a greengrocers on two separate days. The order for each day (in specified units of weight) is given in the matrix below.

$$\begin{array}{c} \\ \text{day 1} \\ \text{day 2} \end{array} \begin{array}{ccc} \textit{Potatoes} & \textit{Onions} & \textit{Carrots} \\ \left[\begin{array}{ccc} 5 & 2 & 2 \\ 4 & 3 & 1 \end{array}\right] \end{array}$$

If potatoes cost £0.15 per unit, onions cost £0.16 per unit and carrots cost £0.12 per unit, express these costs in matrix form and hence obtain a matrix giving the total bill for each day.

$$\begin{array}{c} \\ \text{day 1} \\ \text{day 2} \end{array} \begin{array}{ccc} \textit{Potatoes} & \textit{Onions} & \textit{Carrots} \\ \left[\begin{array}{ccc} 5 & 2 & 2 \\ 4 & 3 & 1 \end{array}\right] \end{array} \qquad \begin{array}{c} \\ \text{Potatoes} \\ \text{Onions} \\ \text{Carrots} \end{array} \begin{array}{c} \textit{Cost (£)} \\ \left[\begin{array}{c} 0.15 \\ 0.16 \\ 0.12 \end{array}\right] \end{array}$$

multiplying these matrices gives:

$$\begin{array}{cc} & \textit{Cost (£)} \\ \left[\begin{array}{ccc} 5 & 2 & 2 \\ 4 & 3 & 1 \end{array}\right] \times \left[\begin{array}{c} 0.15 \\ 0.16 \\ 0.12 \end{array}\right] = \begin{array}{c} \text{day 1} \\ \text{day 2} \end{array} \left[\begin{array}{c} 1.31 \\ 1.20 \end{array}\right] \end{array}$$

7. The Identity matrix

The identity (or unit) matrix is a square matrix having every element zero except the leading diagonal which consists entirely of ones. The identity matrix is denoted by I.

Multiplication of any matrix by I leaves the matrix unchanged

(i.e. Consider a Matrix A, then $AI = IA = A$)

That is:

$$I = \left[\begin{array}{cc} 1 & 0 \\ 0 & 1 \end{array}\right] \qquad I = \left[\begin{array}{ccc} 1 & 0 & 0 \\ 0 & 1 & 0 \\ 0 & 0 & 1 \end{array}\right] \qquad \text{etc.}$$

Example

$$A = \left[\begin{array}{cc} 2 & 3 \\ 0 & -2 \end{array}\right] \qquad B = \left[\begin{array}{ccc} 1 & 0 & 1 \\ 2 & 1 & 0 \end{array}\right]$$

$$AI = \left[\begin{array}{cc} 2 & 3 \\ 0 & -2 \end{array}\right]\left[\begin{array}{cc} 1 & 0 \\ 0 & 1 \end{array}\right] = \left[\begin{array}{cc} 2 & 3 \\ 0 & -2 \end{array}\right]$$

$$IA = \left[\begin{array}{cc} 1 & 0 \\ 0 & 1 \end{array}\right]\left[\begin{array}{cc} 2 & 3 \\ 0 & -2 \end{array}\right] = \left[\begin{array}{cc} 2 & 3 \\ 0 & -2 \end{array}\right]$$

$$BI = \left[\begin{array}{ccc} 1 & 0 & 1 \\ 2 & 1 & 0 \end{array}\right]\left[\begin{array}{ccc} 1 & 0 & 0 \\ 0 & 1 & 0 \\ 0 & 0 & 1 \end{array}\right] = \left[\begin{array}{ccc} 1 & 0 & 1 \\ 2 & 1 & 0 \end{array}\right]$$

Similarly, $IB = B$

8. The Inverse

The inverse of a matrix A is denoted by A^{-1} and is defined as follows:

If the matrix A has an inverse A^{-1} then:

$$AA^{-1} = A^{-1}A = I$$

Any matrix has an inverse if and only if

i) The matrix is square.

ii) The determinant of the matrix is non–zero (i.e. the matrix is non–singular)

The inverse of a matrix A can be calculated using the following formula:

$$A^{-1} = \frac{\text{ADJOINT A}}{|A|}$$

In order to define the *Adjoint* of a square matrix, A, it is first necessary to define some other terms.

$$\text{Let A} = \begin{bmatrix} a & b & c \\ d & e & f \\ g & h & i \end{bmatrix}$$

The *transpose* of A, denoted by A^t, is obtained by writing the rows of A as the columns of A^t.

$$A^t = \begin{bmatrix} a & d & g \\ b & e & h \\ c & f & i \end{bmatrix}$$

Each element of A has a *minor*. The minor of an element is defined as the determinant of the submatrix comprised of the elements which remain when the row and the column of the element in question are deleted.

Each element of A also has a cofactor. The cofactor of the element in row i and column j is the minor of the element in question multiplied by $(-1)^{i+j}$.

The *Adjoint* of A is the matrix of cofactors of A^t. That is, we replace every element of A^t by its cofactor. This is best illustrated by an example.

i) In the case of a matrix of order 2 x 2, the calculation of the inverse is straightforward.

$$\text{If A} = \begin{bmatrix} a & b \\ c & d \end{bmatrix}$$

then immediately we can say

$$A^{-1} = \frac{1}{ad - bc} \begin{bmatrix} d & -b \\ -c & a \end{bmatrix}$$

Example

$$\text{If A} = \begin{bmatrix} 4 & 3 \\ 1 & 2 \end{bmatrix}$$

then a = 4, b = 3, c = 1, d = 2.

$$A^{-1} = \frac{1}{ad-bc} \begin{bmatrix} d & -b \\ -c & a \end{bmatrix}$$

$$A^{-1} = \frac{1}{5} \begin{bmatrix} 2 & -3 \\ -1 & 4 \end{bmatrix}$$

ii) The calculation of the inverse of a matrix of order 3×3 is not so straightforward and is illustrated in the following example.

Example

Consider the following 3×3 matrix and calculate the inverse.

$$A = \begin{bmatrix} 1 & 2 & 2 \\ 3 & -1 & 4 \\ 3 & 2 & -1 \end{bmatrix}$$

step 1: Calculate $|A|$

$$|A| = 1 \begin{vmatrix} -1 & 4 \\ 2 & -1 \end{vmatrix} - 2 \begin{vmatrix} 3 & 4 \\ 3 & -1 \end{vmatrix} + 2 \begin{vmatrix} 3 & -1 \\ 3 & 2 \end{vmatrix}$$

$$= 1(1-8) - 2(-3-12) + 2(6+3)$$

$$= -7 + 30 + 18$$

$$= 41$$

step 2: Calculate the *transpose* of the matrix A (denoted by A^t)

$$A^t = \begin{bmatrix} 1 & 3 & 3 \\ 2 & -1 & 2 \\ 2 & 4 & -1 \end{bmatrix}$$

step 3: Calculate the *Adjoint* of A

$$\text{Adj } A = \begin{bmatrix} +\begin{vmatrix} -1 & 2 \\ 4 & -1 \end{vmatrix} & -\begin{vmatrix} 2 & 2 \\ 2 & -1 \end{vmatrix} & +\begin{vmatrix} 2 & -1 \\ 2 & 4 \end{vmatrix} \\ -\begin{vmatrix} 3 & 3 \\ 4 & -1 \end{vmatrix} & +\begin{vmatrix} 1 & 3 \\ 2 & -1 \end{vmatrix} & -\begin{vmatrix} 1 & 3 \\ 2 & 4 \end{vmatrix} \\ +\begin{vmatrix} 3 & 3 \\ -1 & 2 \end{vmatrix} & -\begin{vmatrix} 1 & 3 \\ 2 & 2 \end{vmatrix} & +\begin{vmatrix} 1 & 3 \\ 2 & -1 \end{vmatrix} \end{bmatrix} = \begin{bmatrix} -7 & 6 & 10 \\ 15 & -7 & 2 \\ 9 & 4 & -7 \end{bmatrix}$$

step 4: Calculate the inverse

$$A^{-1} = \frac{\text{ADJ } A}{|A|} = \frac{1}{41} \begin{bmatrix} -7 & 6 & 10 \\ 15 & -7 & 2 \\ 9 & 4 & -7 \end{bmatrix}$$

8.1 Gaussian Elimination

This provides us with an alternative method for finding the inverse of a matrix. To calculate the inverse of a square matrix A, it is first necessary to set up a tableau of the form

$$[A \,|\, I]$$

where I is the identity matrix, and then to perform a series of row operations to both sides of the partition.

The row operations are aimed at transforming the matrix A to the identity matrix, and hence obtaining the required inverse on the right hand side of the partition. i.e. a tableau of the form

$$[\,I \mid A^{-1}\,]$$

The method is illustrated below on a 2×2 matrix.

Example

Consider $A = \begin{bmatrix} 3 & 4 \\ 2 & 3 \end{bmatrix}$

To calculate the inverse using Gaussian Elimination we proceed as follows:

$$\left[\begin{array}{cc|cc} 3 & 4 & 1 & 0 \\ 2 & 3 & 0 & 1 \end{array}\right]$$

$$\left[\begin{array}{cc|cc} 1 & {}^{4}/_{3} & {}^{1}/_{3} & 0 \\ 2 & 3 & 0 & 1 \end{array}\right] \cdots\cdots\cdots \text{Row } 1 \div 3$$

$$\left[\begin{array}{cc|cc} 1 & {}^{4}/_{3} & {}^{1}/_{3} & 0 \\ 0 & {}^{1}/_{3} & {}^{-1}/_{3} & 1 \end{array}\right] \cdots\cdots\cdots \text{Row } 2 - 2(\text{Row } 1)$$

$$\left[\begin{array}{cc|cc} 1 & {}^{4}/_{3} & {}^{1}/_{3} & 0 \\ 0 & 1 & -2 & 3 \end{array}\right] \cdots\cdots\cdots 3(\text{Row } 2)$$

$$\left[\begin{array}{cc|cc} 1 & 0 & 3 & -4 \\ 0 & 1 & -2 & 3 \end{array}\right] \cdots\cdots\cdots \text{Row } 1 - \tfrac{4}{3}(\text{Row } 2)$$

This tableau is now of the required form so we can say that the inverse of A is:

$$A^{-1} = \begin{bmatrix} 3 & -4 \\ -2 & 3 \end{bmatrix}$$

Exercises (*Answers on page 29*)

1. Evaluate the following determinants

a) $\begin{vmatrix} 2 & 1 \\ 2 & 3 \end{vmatrix}$ b) $\begin{vmatrix} 5 & 4 \\ 3 & 2 \end{vmatrix}$ c) $\begin{vmatrix} -1 & -2 \\ -4 & 3 \end{vmatrix}$

d) $\begin{vmatrix} 1 & 2 & 1 \\ 3 & 1 & 2 \\ 2 & 4 & 3 \end{vmatrix}$ e) $\begin{vmatrix} 2 & -1 & -1 \\ 1 & 3 & 2 \\ 4 & 4 & -1 \end{vmatrix}$

f) $\begin{vmatrix} 0 & -3 & 1 \\ 4 & -2 & 3 \\ 2 & 0 & 4 \end{vmatrix}$

2. Consider the following matrices

$$A = \begin{bmatrix} 2 & 1 \\ 1 & 0 \end{bmatrix} \quad B = \begin{bmatrix} 1 & 1 \\ 0 & 2 \\ 3 & 1 \end{bmatrix}$$

$$C = \begin{bmatrix} 4 & 1 & 0 \\ 1 & 2 & 1 \end{bmatrix} \quad D = \begin{bmatrix} -1 & 3 \\ 2 & -4 \\ -6 & 1 \end{bmatrix}$$

Calculate the following where possible.

a) B + D   b) D + B

c) B + C   d) 4C

e) 5(B + D)   f) A + B

g) AB   h) BA

i) DA   j) BC

k) 8CB   l) B – 3D

m) CD – 7A   n) AC

3. A building contractor is building houses on three different sites. The contractor specialises in three different types of house and the number to be started on each site during the following week are given in the matrix below:

		Site		
		A	B	C
House Type	X	8	7	4
	Y	5	4	5
	Z	3	0	10

In order to start building, the contractor places an initial order for bricks and cement. The amount of bricks and cement ordered (in prearranged batch sizes) for each house type is given in the matrix below.

		Bricks	Cement
House Type	X	10	16
	Y	12	16
	Z	14	17

Obtain a matrix giving the number of batches of bricks and cement that will be delivered to each site.

4. The prices charged by a retailer for five items are given below (in £), in matrix form, for 1989 and 1990

		Item			
	1	2	3	4	5
1989	(2.10	1.20	1.50	0.70	1.00)
1990	(2.50	1.50	1.80	0.75	1.20)

The numbers of each item sold in 1989 and 1990 are as follows (in '000)

			Item		
	1	2	3	4	5
1989	12	16	8	7	9
1990	12	10	11	9	8

Using matrix multiplication. obtain the retailer's revenue (with respect to these five items) for 1989 and 1990 and hence express as a percentage the retailer's increase in revenue in 1990 compared with 1989.

5. Calculate the inverse of the following matrices.

a) $\begin{bmatrix} 3 & 1 \\ 1 & 4 \end{bmatrix}$ b) $\begin{bmatrix} 2 & 4 \\ 5 & 3 \end{bmatrix}$ c) $\begin{bmatrix} -2 & 1 \\ 0 & -3 \end{bmatrix}$

d) $\begin{bmatrix} 1 & 0 & 1 \\ 2 & 3 & 0 \\ 0 & 1 & 2 \end{bmatrix}$ e) $\begin{bmatrix} 2 & 3 & 1 \\ -1 & 0 & 2 \\ 2 & -3 & 0 \end{bmatrix}$

f) $\begin{bmatrix} -2 & 0 & 1 \\ 4 & -3 & 2 \\ 0 & 2 & 1 \end{bmatrix}$

6. Consider the following matrices:

$A = \begin{bmatrix} 2 & 3 \\ 1 & 0 \end{bmatrix}$ $B = \begin{bmatrix} 1 & 2 & 0 \\ 0 & -1 & -2 \end{bmatrix}$

$C = \begin{bmatrix} 4 & 1 \\ 2 & 6 \\ -1 & 0 \end{bmatrix}$

Calculate the following, where possible

i) $(BC)^t$ ii) $(BC)^{-1}$ iii) $(CB)^{-1}$ iv) $(AB)^{-1}$

v) $(CA)^t$ vi) $(BC - A)^{-1}$ vii) $(CA)^t - 4B$ viii) $4AC$

7. The following matrix gives the vitamin contents of three food items, in conveniently chosen units

Vitamin	A	B	C	D
Food I	0.5	0.5	0	0
Food II	0.3	0	0.2	0.1
Food III	0.1	0.1	0.2	0.5

If we eat 5 units of food I, 10 units of food II and 8 units of food III how much of each type of vitamin have we consumed? If we pay only for the vitamin content of each food, paying 10 pence, 20 pence, 25 pence and 50 pence respectively, for units of the four vitamins, how much does a unit of each type of food cost? Compute the total cost of the food eaten. Express the calculations and answers in matrix form.

8. A product is made in three different grades. Each grade is made up of components, A, B, C, D and E as shown in the matrix below:–

		Grades		
		1	2	3
Components	A	1	3	5
	B	3	0	2
	C	2	1	0
	D	5	2	1
	E	0	2	3

The quantities of each grade ordered by customers 1, 2, 3 and 4 for the three grades are shown in the matrix below:–

		Grades		
		1	2	3
Customers	1	3	6	10
	2	4	1	0
	3	5	4	3
	4	4	6	8

a) Arrange these two matrices in a form in which they can be multiplied together. Multiply them, and interpret the resulting matrix.

b) If components A, B, C, D and E cost 15, 10, 9, 5 and 4 pence each respectively, display these figures as a cost vector. Display this cost vector and the matrix obtained in (a) so that they could be multiplied together. Without multiplying them together say what the interpretation of the resulting matrix would be.

9. Work through the following example:

Information provided:

The following tables give the volume of output for three commodities at two factories and the cost per period per commodity at the two factories (in arbitrary units of output and cost).

Table 1: Level of Output

Commodity	A	B	C
Factory 1	6	7	2
Factory 2	4	3	1

Table 2: Cost of output

Quarter	1	2	3	4
Commodity A	2	1	2	1
Commodity B	1	2	2	1
Commodity C	3	3	2	1

You are required to:–

i) Present the information given in Table 1 in matrix notation thus:

$P =$

ii) Present the information given in Table 2 in matrix notation thus:

$C =$

iii) Obtain the matrix product

$PC =$

$= T$

Interpret its meaning and construct a table to present the information so obtained.

iv) Obtain the matrix product

$C^t P^t =$

and verify that this is in fact equal to T^t.

Present this matrix product in tabular form and interpret its meaning.

Short Answers

1. a) 4

    b) −2

    c) −11

    d) −5

    e) −23

    f) 34

2. a) $B + D = \begin{bmatrix} 0 & 4 \\ 2 & -2 \\ -3 & 2 \end{bmatrix}$

    b) D + B = B + D (see a))

    c) Not possible

    d) $\begin{bmatrix} 16 & 4 & 0 \\ 4 & 8 & 4 \end{bmatrix}$

    e) $\begin{bmatrix} 0 & 20 \\ 10 & -10 \\ -15 & 10 \end{bmatrix}$

    f) Not possible

    g) Not possible

    h) $\begin{bmatrix} 3 & 1 \\ 2 & 0 \\ 7 & 3 \end{bmatrix}$

    i) $\begin{bmatrix} 1 & -1 \\ 0 & 2 \\ -11 & -6 \end{bmatrix}$

    j) $\begin{bmatrix} 5 & 3 & 1 \\ 2 & 4 & 2 \\ 13 & 5 & 1 \end{bmatrix}$

    k) $\begin{bmatrix} 32 & 48 \\ 32 & 48 \end{bmatrix}$

    l) $\begin{bmatrix} 4 & -8 \\ -6 & 14 \\ 21 & -2 \end{bmatrix}$

    m) $\begin{bmatrix} -16 & 1 \\ -10 & -4 \end{bmatrix}$

    n) $\begin{bmatrix} 9 & 4 & 1 \\ 4 & 1 & 0 \end{bmatrix}$

3.

	Bricks	Cement
A	182	259
site B	118	176
C	240	314

4. 1989: Revenue = £70.3 (in '000) = £70,300

    1990: Revenue = £81.15 (in '000) = £81,150

    Increase in revenue = £10,850

    Expressed as a % increase = 15.43%

5. a) $\frac{1}{11} \begin{bmatrix} 4 & -1 \\ -1 & 3 \end{bmatrix}$

    b) $-\frac{1}{14} \begin{bmatrix} 3 & -4 \\ -5 & 2 \end{bmatrix}$

    c) $\frac{1}{6} \begin{bmatrix} -3 & -1 \\ 0 & -2 \end{bmatrix}$

    d) $\frac{1}{8} \begin{bmatrix} 6 & 1 & -3 \\ -4 & 2 & 2 \\ 2 & -1 & 3 \end{bmatrix}$

    e) $\frac{1}{27} \begin{bmatrix} 6 & -3 & 6 \\ 4 & -2 & -5 \\ 3 & 12 & 3 \end{bmatrix}$

    f) $\frac{1}{22} \begin{bmatrix} -7 & 2 & 3 \\ -4 & -2 & 8 \\ 8 & 4 & 6 \end{bmatrix}$

6. i) $(BC)^t = \begin{bmatrix} 8 & 0 \\ 13 & -6 \end{bmatrix}$

    ii) $(BC)^{-1} = -\frac{1}{48} \begin{bmatrix} -6 & -13 \\ 0 & 8 \end{bmatrix}$

    iii) $CB = \begin{bmatrix} 4 & 7 & -2 \\ 2 & -2 & -12 \\ -1 & -2 & 0 \end{bmatrix}$

    As CB = 0, therefore CB does not have an inverse.

    iv) (AB) is a 2 x 3 matrix, therefore inverse not possible.

    v) $(CA)^t = \begin{bmatrix} 9 & 10 & -2 \\ 12 & 6 & -3 \end{bmatrix}$

    vi) $(BC - A)^{-1} = -\frac{1}{26} \begin{bmatrix} -6 & -10 \\ 1 & 6 \end{bmatrix}$

    vii) $\begin{bmatrix} 5 & 2 & -2 \\ 12 & 10 & 5 \end{bmatrix}$

    viii) AC not possible

7. Amounts of each vitamin =

$$\begin{array}{cccc} A & B & C & D \end{array}$$
$$\begin{bmatrix} 6.3 & 3.3 & 3.5 & 5.0 \end{bmatrix}$$

Cost (pence) per unit of each food type =

$$\begin{bmatrix} 15 \\ 13 \\ 33 \end{bmatrix} \begin{matrix} I \\ II \\ III \end{matrix}$$

Total cost of food = 469 pence = £4.69

8. a)

$$\begin{matrix} & & Customers \\ & & \begin{matrix} 1 & 2 & 3 & 4 \end{matrix} \end{matrix}$$

$$\text{Components} \begin{matrix} A \\ B \\ C \\ D \\ E \end{matrix} \begin{bmatrix} 71 & 7 & 32 & 62 \\ 29 & 12 & 21 & 28 \\ 12 & 9 & 14 & 14 \\ 37 & 22 & 36 & 40 \\ 42 & 2 & 17 & 36 \end{bmatrix}$$

represents total No. of each type of component ordered by each customer.

b)

$$\begin{array}{ccccc} A & B & C & D & E \end{array}$$
$$\begin{bmatrix} 15 & 10 & 9 & 5 & 4 \end{bmatrix} \text{ pence}$$

$$\begin{bmatrix} 15 & 10 & 9 & 5 & 4 \end{bmatrix} \times \begin{bmatrix} 71 & 7 & 32 & 62 \\ 29 & 12 & 21 & 28 \\ 12 & 9 & 14 & 14 \\ 37 & 22 & 36 & 40 \\ 42 & 2 & 17 & 36 \end{bmatrix}$$

The matrix resulting from this multiplication would give the cost, in pence, to each customer.

9. i) $P = \begin{bmatrix} 6 & 7 & 2 \\ 4 & 3 & 1 \end{bmatrix}$

ii) $C = \begin{bmatrix} 2 & 1 & 2 & 1 \\ 1 & 2 & 2 & 1 \\ 3 & 3 & 2 & 1 \end{bmatrix}$

iii) $PC = \begin{bmatrix} 25 & 26 & 30 & 15 \\ 14 & 13 & 16 & 8 \end{bmatrix}$ gives cost per quarter at each factory

iv) $C^t P^t = \begin{bmatrix} 25 & 14 \\ 26 & 13 \\ 30 & 16 \\ 15 & 8 \end{bmatrix}$

costs:

$$\begin{matrix} & Factory \\ & \begin{matrix} 1 & 2 \end{matrix} \end{matrix}$$

$$\text{Quarter} \begin{matrix} 1 \\ 2 \\ 3 \\ 4 \end{matrix} \begin{bmatrix} 25 & 14 \\ 26 & 13 \\ 30 & 16 \\ 15 & 8 \end{bmatrix}$$

4 Matrix Applications

Simultaneous Linear Equations: Solution and Formulation

1. Introduction

This chapter further develops the concepts introduced in chapter 3. Systems of linear equations are introduced and these are developed to consider both the solution of a set of simultaneous linear equations using matrix methods and also the formulation of a system of linear equations, from given information, to algebraically represent a given problem. This, in itself, provides an introduction to the concepts of 'mathematical modelling' (see section 4) which has a very wide range of applications in business mathematics and operational research.

2. Simultaneous Linear Equations

The solution of a system of linear equations means the establishment of a value for each of the variables in the system which satisfies all the equations simultaneously.

Consider a system of equations with n unknowns (i.e. n variables).

The requirements for a unique solution are:

i) There are n equations.

ii) The n equations are independent.

iii) The n equations are consistent.

Example

$$x + y + z = 3$$
$$2x - y - 3z = 4$$

This is a system of two simultaneous linear equations with three unknowns. This system does not have a unique solution as requirement (i), above, is not satisfied.

Example

$$2x + y = 5 \dots\dots\dots\dots (1)$$
$$4x + 2y = 10 \dots\dots\dots (2)$$

This is a system of two simultaneous linear equations with two unknowns. However, equation (2) is a multiple of equation (1) [i.e. equation (2) = 2 x equation (1)], therefore the equations are not independent, and the system does not have a unique solution as requirement (ii), above, is not satisfied.

Example

$$x + y = 3 \ldots\ldots\ldots (3)$$

$$2x + 2y = 7 \ldots\ldots\ldots (4)$$

Again, this is a system with two equations and two unknowns. However, these equations are inconsistent [2 x equation (3) contradicts equation (4)] and hence there is no unique solution as requirement (iii), above, is not satisfied.

3. Solution by matrices

There are a number of methods for solving a set of linear equations. In this section the solution of a set of linear equations using matrices is introduced.

Generally, a system of n simultaneous linear equations in n unknowns can be expressed in a matrix form as:

$$A \underline{x} = \underline{b}$$

where   A is a square matrix of order n x n

and $\underline{x}$, $\underline{b}$ are column vectors of order n x 1

A system of linear equations expressed in the form $A \underline{x} = \underline{b}$ has a unique solution if and only if A is nonsingular (i.e. A is square and $|A| \neq 0$). This condition corresponds with the requirements given in section 1.

The method of solution is as follows:

$$A \underline{x} = \underline{b}$$
$$A^{-1}A \underline{x} = A^{-1} \underline{b}$$
$$I \underline{x} = A^{-1} \underline{b}$$
$$\underline{x} = A^{-1} \underline{b}$$

Example

To solve the following system of equations

$$x + 2y + 2z = 4$$

$$3x - y + 4z = 25$$

$$3x + 2y - z = -4$$

we first express them in matrix form as:

$$\begin{bmatrix} 1 & 2 & 2 \\ 3 & -1 & 4 \\ 3 & 2 & -1 \end{bmatrix} \begin{bmatrix} x \\ y \\ z \end{bmatrix} = \begin{bmatrix} 4 \\ 25 \\ -4 \end{bmatrix}$$

where $A = \begin{bmatrix} 1 & 2 & 2 \\ 3 & -1 & 4 \\ 3 & 2 & -1 \end{bmatrix}$

$$\underline{x} = \begin{bmatrix} x \\ y \\ z \end{bmatrix}$$

$$\underline{b} = \begin{bmatrix} 4 \\ 25 \\ -4 \end{bmatrix}$$

Now:

$$A^{-1} = \frac{1}{41} \begin{bmatrix} -7 & 6 & 10 \\ 15 & -7 & 2 \\ 9 & 4 & -7 \end{bmatrix} \text{ (see previous unit)}$$

The solution is given by:

$$\underline{x} = A^{-1} \underline{b}$$

$$\underline{x} = \frac{1}{41} \begin{bmatrix} -7 & 6 & 10 \\ 15 & -7 & 2 \\ 9 & 4 & -7 \end{bmatrix} \begin{bmatrix} 4 \\ 25 \\ -4 \end{bmatrix}$$

$$\underline{x} = \frac{1}{41} \begin{bmatrix} 82 \\ -123 \\ 164 \end{bmatrix}$$

$$\text{i.e. } \begin{bmatrix} x \\ y \\ z \end{bmatrix} = \begin{bmatrix} 2 \\ -3 \\ 4 \end{bmatrix}$$

Hence the solution is $x = 2, \ y = -3, \ z = 4$

Example

Solve the following system of equations:

$$2x + y = 2$$
$$z - 4y = 0$$
$$4x + z = 6$$

Rearranging, this system becomes:

$$2x + y \quad = 2$$
$$\quad -4y + z = 0$$
$$4x \quad + z = 6$$

In matrix form:

$$\begin{bmatrix} 2 & 1 & 0 \\ 0 & -4 & 1 \\ 4 & 0 & 1 \end{bmatrix} \begin{bmatrix} x \\ y \\ z \end{bmatrix} = \begin{bmatrix} 2 \\ 0 \\ 6 \end{bmatrix}$$

$$A = \begin{bmatrix} 2 & 1 & 0 \\ 0 & -4 & 1 \\ 4 & 0 & 1 \end{bmatrix}$$

$$|A| = 2(-4) - 1(-4) + 0$$

$$= -4$$

$$A^t = \begin{bmatrix} 2 & 0 & 4 \\ 1 & -4 & 0 \\ 0 & 1 & 1 \end{bmatrix} \qquad \text{Adj } A = \begin{bmatrix} +\begin{vmatrix} -4 & 0 \\ 1 & 1 \end{vmatrix} & -\begin{vmatrix} 1 & 0 \\ 0 & 1 \end{vmatrix} & +\begin{vmatrix} 1 & -4 \\ 0 & 1 \end{vmatrix} \\ -\begin{vmatrix} 0 & 4 \\ 1 & 1 \end{vmatrix} & +\begin{vmatrix} 2 & 4 \\ 0 & 1 \end{vmatrix} & -\begin{vmatrix} 2 & 0 \\ 0 & 1 \end{vmatrix} \\ +\begin{vmatrix} 0 & 4 \\ -4 & 0 \end{vmatrix} & -\begin{vmatrix} 2 & 4 \\ 1 & 0 \end{vmatrix} & +\begin{vmatrix} 2 & 0 \\ 1 & -4 \end{vmatrix} \end{bmatrix}$$

$$A^{-1} = -\frac{1}{4} \begin{bmatrix} -4 & -1 & 1 \\ 4 & 2 & -2 \\ 16 & 4 & -8 \end{bmatrix}$$

Now:

$$\underline{x} = A^{-1}\underline{b}$$

$$\underline{x} = -\frac{1}{4} \begin{bmatrix} -4 & -1 & 1 \\ 4 & 2 & -2 \\ 16 & 4 & -8 \end{bmatrix} \begin{bmatrix} 2 \\ 0 \\ 6 \end{bmatrix} = -\frac{1}{4} \begin{bmatrix} -2 \\ -4 \\ -16 \end{bmatrix}$$

$$\underline{x} = \begin{bmatrix} {}^1/_2 \\ 1 \\ 4 \end{bmatrix}$$

Hence $x = {}^1/_2$, $y = 1$, $z = 4$

4. Formulation of a Problem

A 'mathematical model' is a representation of a real–life situation in mathematical terms. Such a representation may be fairly straightforward (eg by one or more linear equations) or alternatively may be very complex, depending upon the situation being modelled.

Consider the following example:

Question

A firm manufactures three metal alloys, A, B, and C. These require machining and the machining capacity is 86 hours per week.

    Alloy A requires 3 machine hours per tonne for processing

    Alloy B requires 4 machine hours per tonne for processing

    Alloy C requires 2 machine hours per tonne for processing

Each alloy requires the addition of a particular metal of which 186 Kgs are available per week.

    Alloy A requires 3 Kgs per tonne of this metal

    Alloy B requires 9 Kgs per tonne of this metal

    Alloy C requires 6 Kgs per tonne of this metal

Time is also required to harden the alloys in a furnace. Furnace capacity is 128 hours per week.

    A requires 4 hours per tonne in the furnace

    B requires 7 hours per tonne in the furnace

    C requires 3 hours per tonne in the furnace

Calculate the quantities of the metal alloys which can be produced each week so that all the available resources are fully used.

Solution

To represent this situation in mathematical terms we proceed as follows:

Let x be the quantities (in tonnes) produced per week of Alloy A

   y be the quantities (in tonnes) produced per week of Alloy B

   z be the quantities (in tonnes) produced per week of Alloy C

Expressing the information given in tableau form:

		Alloys		*Maximum*
	A	*B*	*C*	*Available*
Processing time	3	4	2	86
Metal requirement	3	9	6	186
Furnace time	4	7	3	128

The resulting equations are as follows:

Processing time equation (hrs):

From the table above it can be seen that the total number of machine hours used for processing in the production of x of alloy A, y of alloy B, and z of alloy C is given by:

$$3x + 4y + 2z$$

As the total hours available for processing equal 86, we thus have our first equation (assuming all of these hours are used) which is:

Processing time equation (hrs): $3x + 4y + 2z = 86$

Similarly we can obtain the other two equations as follows:

Metal requirement equation (Kgs): $3x + 9y + 6z = 186$

Furnace time equation (hrs): $4x + 7y + 3z = 128$

In matrix notation we have:

$$\begin{pmatrix} 3 & 4 & 2 \\ 3 & 9 & 6 \\ 4 & 7 & 3 \end{pmatrix} \begin{pmatrix} x \\ y \\ z \end{pmatrix} = \begin{pmatrix} 86 \\ 186 \\ 128 \end{pmatrix}$$

Now:

$A \underline{x} = \underline{b}$, which has a solution given by $\underline{x} = A^{-1}\underline{b}$

where $A^{-1} = \dfrac{Adj\,A}{|A|}$

and we have:

$$A = \begin{bmatrix} 3 & 4 & 2 \\ 3 & 9 & 6 \\ 4 & 7 & 3 \end{bmatrix}$$

$$|A| = 3 \begin{vmatrix} 9 & 6 \\ 7 & 3 \end{vmatrix} - 4 \begin{vmatrix} 3 & 6 \\ 4 & 3 \end{vmatrix} + 2 \begin{vmatrix} 3 & 9 \\ 4 & 7 \end{vmatrix}$$

$$= 3(27 - 42) - 4(9 - 24) + 2(21 - 36)$$

$$= -45 + 60 - 30$$

$$= -15$$

$$A^t = \begin{bmatrix} 3 & 3 & 4 \\ 4 & 9 & 7 \\ 2 & 6 & 3 \end{bmatrix} \quad \text{Adj } A = \begin{bmatrix} -15 & 2 & 6 \\ 15 & 1 & -12 \\ -15 & -5 & 15 \end{bmatrix} \quad A^{-1} = \frac{-1}{15} \begin{bmatrix} -15 & 2 & 6 \\ 15 & 1 & -12 \\ -15 & -5 & 15 \end{bmatrix}$$

Hence, using $\underline{x} = A^{-1}\underline{b}$, we have

$$\begin{bmatrix} x \\ y \\ z \end{bmatrix} = -\frac{1}{15} \begin{bmatrix} -15 & 2 & 6 \\ 15 & 1 & -12 \\ -15 & -5 & 15 \end{bmatrix} \begin{bmatrix} 86 \\ 186 \\ 128 \end{bmatrix}$$

$$= -\frac{1}{15} \begin{bmatrix} -1290 & 372 & 768 \\ 1290 & 186 & -1586 \\ -1290 & -930 & 1920 \end{bmatrix} = \begin{bmatrix} 10 \\ 4 \\ 20 \end{bmatrix}$$

The solution is $x = 10$; $y = 4$; $z = 20$;

Hence, when all resources are to be used up, production per week should be:

Alloy A = 10 tonnes; Alloy B = 4 tonnes; Alloy C = 20 tonnes

 Exercises (Answers on page 41)

1. Calculate the inverse of

    $$A = \begin{bmatrix} 1 & 2 & 3 \\ 2 & 3 & 2 \\ 3 & 3 & 4 \end{bmatrix}$$

    and show that:

    $$A^{-1}A = \begin{bmatrix} 1 & 0 & 0 \\ 0 & 1 & 0 \\ 0 & 0 & 1 \end{bmatrix} = AA^{-1}$$

2. Investigate whether or not the following systems have a unique solution and solve for x, y and z when possible.

    a) $x + 2y + 2z = 2$

    $2x + 4y + z = -1$

    $3x + 6y + 5z = 2$

    b) $6x - 2y + z = 1$

    $x - 4y + 2z = 0$

    $4x + 6y - 3z = 0$

    c) $2x + 3y - 4z = 1$

    $3x - y + 2z = -2$

    $5x - 9y - 4z = 3$

3. Solve:

$$\begin{bmatrix} 1 & 2 & 3 \\ 4 & -1 & 0 \\ 3 & 2 & -1 \end{bmatrix} \begin{bmatrix} x \\ y \\ z \end{bmatrix} = \begin{bmatrix} 13 \\ 1 \\ 7 \end{bmatrix}$$

4. a) For the following matrices,

$$P = \begin{bmatrix} 4 & 2 \\ 2 & 1 \\ 1 & 3 \end{bmatrix} \qquad Q = \begin{bmatrix} 3 & 2 & 1 \\ 4 & 0 & 2 \end{bmatrix}$$

$$R = \begin{bmatrix} 4 & 3 \\ 2 & 1 \end{bmatrix} \qquad S = \begin{bmatrix} 3 & 1 & 2 \\ 5 & 3 & 4 \end{bmatrix}$$

   Compute, if possible:

   i) $P - S$

   ii) $\frac{1}{3}(Q + S)$

   iii) $R \times Q$

   iv) $P \times R$

   v) The inverse matrix of P

   vi) $R^{-1} \times S$

   b) Express the following set of linear equations in matrix form and state the steps required to solve for x, y and z using matrix methods, *but without actually doing the calculation.*

   $$x + 2y + z = 1$$
   $$2x - y + 2z = 7$$
   $$x + y - z = 0$$

5. a) State the conditions under which a system of equations with n unknowns has a unique solution.

   b) A firm manufactures three items of furniture. Each requires a number of different types of wood. The most expensive types of wood used are chipboard, agba and beech and each item's requirements of these are given in the following table (in units of 1000 sq. cm.)

	Chipboard	Agba	Beech
Item A	12.5	2.5	3.75
Item B	10	1.25	2.5
Item C	15	3.75	3.75

   Chipboard costs the firm £0.4 per 1000 sq. cm., and both agba and beech costs £0.8 per 1000 sq. cm. If the firm's monthly budget allows for £3200 to be spent on chipboard, £1400 to be spent on agba and £1700 to be spent on beech, how many of each item can be produced per month?

6. A confectionery manufacturer is making up his range of Christmas selection boxes. This year there are to be three types of box, 'Sunny Santa' , 'Red Robin' and the 'Happy Holly'.

   The 'Sunny Santa' contains 6 packets of boiled sweets, 4 bars of chocolate and 2 packets of sweet biscuits. The 'Red Robin' contains 2 packets of sweets, 3 bars of chocolate and 3 packets of biscuits, while the 'Happy Holly' contains 3 packets of sweets, 2 bars of chocolate and 4 packets of biscuits.

The firm has available 90,000 packets of sweets, 66,000 bars of chocolate and 48,000 packets of biscuits, and wishes to use up all of these.

Calculate the number of Christmas selection boxes of each type that can be produced by expressing the problem as a system of linear equations and solving using Matrix algebra.

7. A toy manufacturer uses screws, nails and bolts in the assembly of three models of toys.

The following table shows the number required for each toy.

	Toy A	Toy B	Toy C
Number of screws	6	3	4
Number of nails	5	4	4
Number of bolts	2	1	3

Each screw costs the manufacturer 2p, each nail 1p and each bolt 3p, and the manufacturer's budget allows £38 per month to be spent on screws, £18 per month on nails and £24 per month on bolts.

If this budget is to be met exactly, formulate the above data as a set of linear equations and, using matrix methods, find the number of each model of toy that can be made each month.

8. A small pottery firm specialises in a line of decorated tea mugs which they make in two sizes, large and standard. The Sales Department consider that there would be a sure sale in Jubilee Year for an additional mug, decorated with the Queen's picture, to be called the Jubilee mug. Manufacturing data is as follows:

Labour Hours available per week:

Pottery Moulding	40
Kiln Work	70
Decoration	200

Labour minutes required for 100 mugs:

	Large	Standard	Jubilee
Pottery Moulding	20	10	10
Kiln work	20	20	20
Decoration	60	40	80

Formulate the data as a series of linear equations and using matrix methods find the number of different types of mug that can be made per week so that all the available labour is utilised.

9. Complete the following example.

A manufacturer wishes to examine a factory's production costs and utilisation of resources with a view to adding to his stock of three particular products. The following table gives information on three specific inputs required for the production of X_1, X_2, and X_3 units of products 1, 2 and 3 respectively.

Type of input	Requirements per unit of output for each product			Availability (Max)
	1	2	3	
Machine hours	5	6	9	44 hours
Labour hours	2	4	7	31 hours
Raw material units	3	2	5	22 hours
Cost of unit output (in £)	72	60	85	

i) On the assumption that the manufacturer wishes to attain an output which uses up all of the available resources, verify that this objective requires the solution of the following system of simultaneous equations:

$$5X_1 + 6X_2 + 9X_3 = 44$$

$$2X_1 + 4X_2 + 7X_3 = 31$$

$$3X_1 + 2X_2 + 5X_3 = 22$$

and that this may be represented in matrix notation as:

$$\begin{bmatrix} 5 & 6 & 9 \\ 2 & 4 & 7 \\ 3 & 2 & 5 \end{bmatrix} \begin{bmatrix} X_1 \\ X_2 \\ X_3 \end{bmatrix} = \begin{bmatrix} 44 \\ 31 \\ 22 \end{bmatrix}$$

and that this is of the general form:

$$A\underline{x} = \underline{b}$$

for which the solution is:

$$\underline{x} = A^{-1}\underline{b}$$

ii) Calculate the determinant of the matrix A

iii) Verify that the transpose of the matrix A is given by:

$$A^t = \begin{bmatrix} 5 & 2 & 3 \\ 6 & 4 & 2 \\ 9 & 7 & 5 \end{bmatrix}$$

and hence calculate the Adjoint of the Matrix A by completing the following:

$$\text{Adj } A = \begin{bmatrix} +\begin{vmatrix} 4 & 2 \\ 7 & 5 \end{vmatrix} & -\begin{vmatrix} 6 & 2 \\ 9 & 5 \end{vmatrix} & +\begin{vmatrix} 6 & 4 \\ 9 & 7 \end{vmatrix} \\ -\begin{vmatrix} 2 & 3 \\ 7 & 5 \end{vmatrix} & +\begin{vmatrix} & \\ & \end{vmatrix} & -\begin{vmatrix} & \\ & \end{vmatrix} \\ +\begin{vmatrix} & \\ & \end{vmatrix} & -\begin{vmatrix} & \\ & \end{vmatrix} & +\begin{vmatrix} & \\ & \end{vmatrix} \end{bmatrix}$$

$$= \begin{bmatrix} 6 & -12 & 6 \\ 11 & & \end{bmatrix}$$

It is recommended that you should first verify that the entries provided in these matrices are correct before you continue with the required calculations.

iv) Check the accuracy of your calculations by obtaining the matrix product:

$$(\text{Adj A}) \times A = \begin{bmatrix} 6 & -12 & 6 \\ 11 & & \\ & & \end{bmatrix} \begin{bmatrix} 5 & 6 & 9 \\ 2 & 4 & 7 \\ 3 & 2 & 5 \end{bmatrix}$$

and establish that this is fact is equal to:

$$(\text{Adj A}) \times A = |A| \begin{bmatrix} 1 & 0 & 0 \\ 0 & 1 & 0 \\ 0 & 0 & 1 \end{bmatrix}$$

v) Obtain the solution to the problem by completing the following:

$$\begin{bmatrix} x_1 \\ x_2 \\ x_3 \end{bmatrix} = \frac{1}{|A|} \begin{bmatrix} 6 & -12 & 6 \\ 11 & & \\ & & \end{bmatrix} \begin{bmatrix} 44 \\ 31 \\ 22 \end{bmatrix}$$

$$= \frac{1}{|A|} \begin{bmatrix} \\ \\ \end{bmatrix} = \begin{bmatrix} \\ \\ \end{bmatrix}$$

vi) Calculate the total cost of production.

10. i) Set up the following system of equations in matrix form ie $A\underline{x} = \underline{b}$

$$4x + 3y + z = 2$$
$$y + z = 2$$
$$x + y + z = 2$$

Identify A, $\underline{x}$ and $\underline{b}$.

Hence solve the equations (using $\underline{x} = A^{-1}\underline{b}$).

ii) Formulate the following information as a system of linear equations but *DO NOT ATTEMPT TO SOLVE* the equations.

A warehouse stocks four types of furniture viz. tables, chairs, wall–units and bookcases. The total number of pieces of furniture stocked equals 500, and the number of chairs equals the sum of the number of tables, wall–units and bookcases. It is also known that the number of tables equals the number of wall–units and, further, that the number of bookcases multiplied by eight equals the sum of the number of tables and wall–units multiplied by two.

11. The monthly supply of a commodity is estimated to be 50,000 tons when the selling price is £10 per ton, and 70,000 when the selling price is £30 per ton. The monthly demand for the commodity is estimated to be 60,000 tons when the buying price is £10 per ton and 40,000 tons when the price is £30 per ton. Assuming that both supply and demand functions are linear in terms of price per ton,

a) Obtain these functions

b) Determine the point of market equilibrium (ie where these functions intersect).

Short Answers

1. $A^{-1} = -\dfrac{1}{7}\begin{bmatrix} 6 & 1 & -5 \\ -2 & -5 & 4 \\ -3 & 3 & -1 \end{bmatrix}$

2. a) No solution

   b) No solution

   c) $\begin{bmatrix} x \\ y \\ z \end{bmatrix} = \dfrac{1}{198}\begin{bmatrix} -68 \\ -50 \\ -121 \end{bmatrix}$

3. $x = 1; y = 3; z = 2$

4. i) Not possible

   ii) $\begin{bmatrix} 2 & 1 & 1 \\ 3 & 1 & 2 \end{bmatrix}$

   iii) $\begin{bmatrix} 24 & 8 & 10 \\ 10 & 4 & 4 \end{bmatrix}$

   iv) $\begin{bmatrix} 20 & 14 \\ 10 & 7 \\ 10 & 6 \end{bmatrix}$

   v) Not possible

   vi) $\begin{bmatrix} 6 & 4 & 5 \\ -7 & -5 & -6 \end{bmatrix}$

5. 200 of A, 100 of B, 300 of C.

6. 12200 of Sunny Santa; 3600 of Red Robin; 3200 of Happy Holly.

7. 200 of A, 100 of B, 100 of C.

8. 3000 Large, 10500 Standard, 7500 Jubilee.

9. $|A| = 24$

   $Adj\ A = \begin{bmatrix} 6 & -12 & 6 \\ 11 & -2 & -17 \\ -8 & 8 & 8 \end{bmatrix}$

   $\begin{bmatrix} x \\ y \\ z \end{bmatrix} = \begin{bmatrix} 1 \\ 2 \\ 3 \end{bmatrix}$

   Therefore we require 1 unit of product 1, 2 units of product 2 and 3 units of product 3.

   The total cost of production = £447

10. $x = 0, y = 0, z = 2$

$$
\begin{aligned}
w + b + c + t &= 500 \\
w + b + t &= c \\
t &= w \\
2(t + w) &= 8b
\end{aligned}
$$

   i.e.

$$
\begin{aligned}
w + b + c + t &= 500 \\
w + b - c + t &= 0 \\
w \qquad\quad - t &= 0 \\
2w - 8b \quad + 2t &= 0
\end{aligned}
$$

11. i) $X_s = 40{,}000 + 1000p$

   $X_d = 70{,}000 - 1000p$

   ii) £15

   55,000.

Part 2
Statistics

Introduction

'Statistics' is concerned with the collection, organisation, presentation and analysis of data. This part of the book consists of nine chapters and the topics covered are those considered essential for all students coming new to the subject. These topics underpin a further, more advanced, study of statistics and its applications.

The first four chapters deal with descriptive statistics, which is concerned with summarizing, describing and presenting data. These chapters also provide a general introduction to statistical terms in common usage in a variety of applications. The next four chapters introduce the basics of probability and probability distributions which also underpin more advanced applications that are very relevant to business - such applications are numerous and include Quality Control and the whole area of statistical testing and inference. The final chapter looks at the study of more than one variable by considering Correlation and Regression, which provides a basis for more advanced applications including business forecasting.

5 | Statistical Diagrams

1. Introduction

It is often useful to present data visually by means of statistical diagrams. Such presentations can emphasise important features of data which would not be obvious from a mass of data or from data presented in tabular form.

Data may be from a *sample* or from a *population*. A population is a set of items of interest in a statistical study, while a sample is a subset of a population.

A very important aspect of all statistical diagrams is accuracy as it should be noted that such diagrams are open to misuse. It is therefore necessary that all such diagrams should be clearly labelled:

i.e.   –   the diagram should have a clear heading

      –   where appropriate axes and/or other component parts of the diagram should be clearly identified (for certain diagrams a 'key' may be useful in this respect)

      –   if appropriate, the units of measurement should be clearly identified

      –   the source of the information or data displayed in the diagram should be given.

Some of the more common types of statistical diagrams are considered here.

2. Pictograms

A very basic form of visual representation, often used to present information to the general public, is the 'pictogram'. A pictogram usually consists of easily recognisable pictures which are used to convey a message simply and which do not require any technical understanding. It is not a very accurate form of diagram and has only limited use in business but, given its purpose, this is not a serious handicap though it can be misused.

Example

The number of people employed at a particular company (as of the 1 January) is provided in the table below.

	No. of employees
1988	3000
1989	3500
1990	4000
1991	4250

This data could be represented as follows:

Diagram 5.1

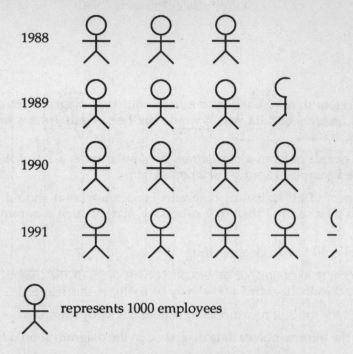

represents 1000 employees

3. Bar Charts

These are a very popular and effective type of diagram which come in a variety of forms. The data is represented by a series of bars which may or may not be subdivided into component parts, and which can be drawn either vertically or horizontally. Examples of different kinds of 'bar chart' are described in the following sections.

3.1 Simple Bar Chart

A 'Simple Bar Chart' depicts the magnitudes of different categories of data by a series of bars. In drawing such a chart the length of the bars are proportional to the magnitude of the categories/items being considered.

Example

The 'Simple Bar Chart' in Diagram 5.2 represents a firm's monthly sales revenue (in £'000) for the first six months of 1990 – as given in the table below.

	Sales Revenue (£'000)
Jan	3.8
Feb	4.1
Mar	4.4
Apr	4.7
May	5.5
Jun	6.2

Diagram 5.2

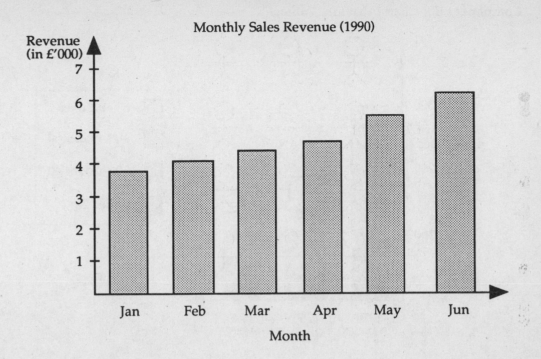

Monthly Sales Revenue (1990)

3.2 Component Bar Charts

These are similar to a simple bar chart except that the bars are subdivided into component parts. The charts considered here can be used to represent the data in absolute terms (usually referred to as simply a 'component bar chart') or in percentage terms (referred to as a 'percentage component bar chart').

Consider the following table which gives the number of employees at a company subdivided into age categories for each of 3 years (as of 1 Jan).

Table 5.3

	Year		
Age	*1970*	*1980*	*1990*
under 20	30 (10%)	40 (20%)	15 (10%)
20 – under 40	150 (50%)	100 (50%)	45 (30%)
40 – under 60	90 (30%)	50 (25%)	75 (50%)
60 and over	30 (10%)	10 (5%)	15 (10%)
Total number of employees	300	200	150

(The percentages represent percentages of the total number of employees for the year in question). This table will be used to illustrate the use of component bar charts.

3.2.1 Component Bar Chart (Absolute Values)

Diagram 5.4

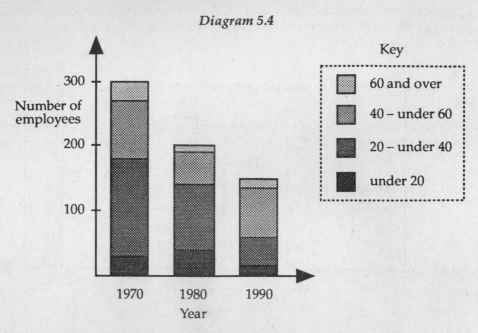

This table allows us to compare component parts as well as totals in absolute terms.

3.2.2 Percentage Component Bar Chart

Diagram 5.5

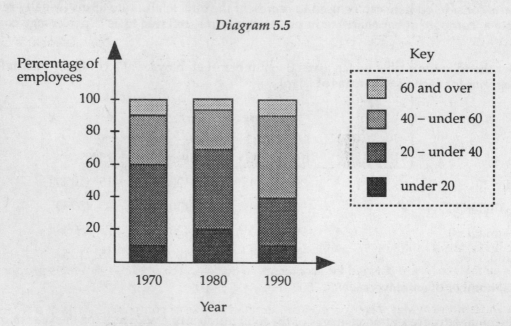

The diagram shows relative comparisons between component parts (the height of each bar is the same ie 100%).

3.3 Multiple Bar Charts

Here the component parts are shown adjoining each other by starting all components at the same base line. This allows a straightforward comparison between several component parts, but the comparison of totals is largely lost.

Example

Consider the following information concerning absenteeism at three factories, A, B, and C, in 1980, 1985 and 1990.

Table 5.6 (below) gives details of the number of working days lost due to absenteeism at each factory for the years in question.

Table 5.6

Company	1980	1985	1990
A	40	40	60
B	20	25	20
C	10	15	35

This can be represented by the following 'Multiple Bar Chart'.

Diagram 5.7

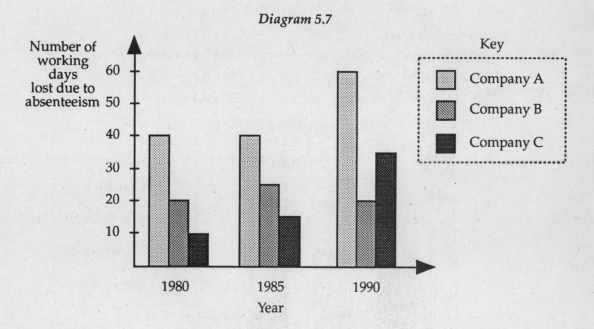

4. Pie Diagrams

This is a circular diagram divided into segments so that the area of each segment is proportional to the component part being represented.

The Pie Diagram provides a comparison of the relative size of component parts of a total, and its construction involves calculation of the angles at the centre of the diagram.

Comparison of the different segments is, however, not always straightforward unless the relevant figures are inserted into the segments.

Example

A company's costs for the last year have been broken down as follows:

	Cost (£'000)
Salaries and wages	500
Equipment costs	200
Raw materials	150
Miscellaneous costs	50
	900

To represent this information by means of a 'pie chart', it is first necessary to calculate the angle at the centre for each segment – this angle being proportional to the item represented. To calculate these angles we first divide 360° by the total cost.

In this example this equals 0.4 (ie $\frac{360}{900}$), and we must now multiply each cost by this value to obtain the required angles. This is illustrated below:

Table 5.8

	Cost (£'000)	Angle
Salaries and wages	500	500 x 0.4 = 200°
Equipment costs	200	200 x 0.4 = 80°
Raw materials	150	150 x 0.4 = 60°
Miscellaneous costs	50	50 x 0.4 = 20°
	900	

Diagram 5.9

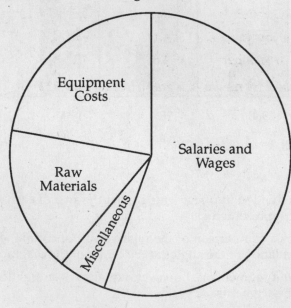

5. Graphs

Graphs are a very useful and common means of presenting data that come in a variety of forms, the simplest of which will be introduced here. A particular advantage of using graphs is that a number of them can be superimposed on the same axes thus enabling certain comparisons to be made very clearly. One frequent application of the use of graphs is a time series which represents the change of a variable over a period of time (eg unemployment figures; Company profits: etc).

It should be noted that care is particularly necessary in labelling and in the choice of axes and units when drawing graphs – lack of care in these respects could lead to a misleading diagram

Example

The following table provides information relating to a company's sales of two products over a 12–month period:

Table 5.10

Sales (£'000)

Month	Product A	Product B
January	3.0	4.8
February	2.5	4.1
March	2.8	3.3
April	3.1	2.9
May	3.4	2.8
June	4.1	2.9
July	4.4	3.4
August	3.7	3.7
September	3.2	3.8
October	3.2	3.9
November	4.1	4.0
December	4.8	4.1

This information is illustrated by means of a graph in Diagram 5.11

Diagram 5.11

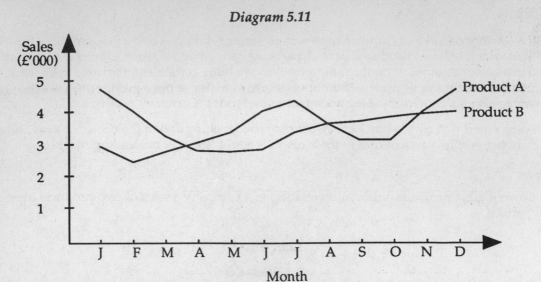

6. Other Diagrams

There are a number of other types of diagrams, charts and graphs which can be used to visually present data, many of which can often be seen in newspapers, periodicals, journals, etc. While all such statistical diagrams can be effective and beneficial, the reader should be aware that they can also be open to abuse by being drawn in a misleading way. Care should therefore be taken when drawing a statistical diagram and also when interpreting one.

Exercises

1. Consider the following table which represents the output of three products from two factories over a period of four years (subdivided into quarters).

		Factory 1 Product			Factory 2 Product		
Year	Qtr	A	B	C	A	B	C
1987	1	3.7	6.0	8.4	6.8	13.0	18.0
	2	3.2	6.2	8.3	6.8	13.6	17.1
	3	3.6	6.3	8.3	7.5	14.0	16.5
	4	3.8	6.7	8.2	8.2	14.2	16.0
1988	1	4.1	6.9	7.9	8.6	14.4	15.8
	2	4.0	7.1	7.4	8.2	14.9	15.3
	3	4.1	7.4	7.4	8.8	15.1	14.7
	4	4.3	7.6	7.3	9.0	15.6	14.2
1989	1	4.5	7.8	7.1	9.4	16.2	13.7
	2	4.1	7.9	7.0	9.2	16.8	13.1
	3	4.4	7.9	6.6	9.6	17.5	12.9
	4	4.8	8.1	6.3	10.0	17.8	12.1
1990	1	5.0	8.2	6.3	10.6	18.4	11.2
	2	4.9	8.3	6.0	10.2	18.7	10.5
	3	5.1	8.5	5.9	10.8	19.1	10.1
	4	5.4	8.9	5.8	11.0	19.5	9.6

Output ('000)

Demonstrate your knowledge of statistical diagrams by graphically representing information from the table on the previous page in a way you think appropriate.

2. Assignment:

    Examine critically the use of statistical charts, diagrams, graphs and tables etc. in newspapers, periodicals and other publications.

    Criteria for assessment:

    i)   You should produce a carefully written report, the length of which should be between 8 – 16 sides, describing the different types of statistical diagrams etc., when they may be used, and how they could be misinterpreted or misrepresented.

    ii) You should make extensive use of examples, in particular examples cut out from news-papers etc., with special reference to those that are open to misinterpretation.

6 Frequency Distributions

1. Introduction

There are many situations where a mass of raw data has been collected (eg surveys, opinion polls, etc) and needs to be analysed and presented. Such a mass of raw data is not usually in a form that can be easily understood and few, if any, conclusions can be drawn from it. Though, in itself, such data is not very meaningful, it may be able to be summarised by constructing a frequency distribution.

2. Frequency Distribution

A frequency distribution is a table listing the possible values of a variable together with the number of observed values associated with each. This is best illustrated by an example.

Example

The following raw data refer to the number of children per family in each of 36 families living in a certain block of flats.

Ground Floor	2	1	0	1	2	2
First Floor	3	4	3	6	3	5
Second Floor	1	0	2	1	4	2
Third Floor	2	3	1	3	1	0
Fourth Floor	5	1	2	3	2	1
Fifth Floor	2	0	3	2	4	2

By listing each figure from 0 to 6 once and writing down, in an adjacent column, the number of times each figure occurs, we can construct a frequency distribution.

No. of children per family	No. of families
0	4
1	8
2	11
3	7
4	3
5	2
6	1

The data is now clearly in a more understandable form, though it should be noted that some information has been lost (i.e. the floor on which each family lives is not displayed in this table).

In this example, the *variable* under consideration is the 'Number of children per family' and the number of times each value of the variable occurs (i.e. the number of families) is called the *frequency*. In general, the values of the variable are listed in order of magnitude in the left–hand column, and the corresponding frequencies are recorded in the right–hand column.

3. Grouped Frequency Distributions

Where the range of values of a variable is large, we can group several values of the variable together to form a grouped frequency distribution.

The variable may be *continuous* with the variable taking any value within a given range (e.g. Height, Weight, etc.) or *discrete* with the variable taking only specific values (e.g. Number of rooms in a house, sizes of shoe, etc.).

Examples of a grouped frequency distribution for a continuous variable and a discrete variable are given below.

Example

A grouped frequency distribution for a continuous variable:

Height of 30 children (in cm)

Height	No. of children
55 – under 60	2
60 – under 65	10
65 – under 70	12
70 – under 75	4
75 and over	2

Example

A grouped frequency distribution for a discrete variable:

Number of cars arriving at a service station each day (over a period of 25 days).

No. of cars	No. of days
30 – 39	5
40 – 49	10
50 – 59	6
60 – 69	3
70 and over	1

When the values of the variable are grouped together the groups formed are generally known as *classes* and a list of such classes, together with their corresponding frequencies, form the grouped frequency distribution. The width of a class is called the *class interval* (i.e. the difference between the *class boundaries*).

The *class boundaries* are the points which are halfway between the upper and lower limits, respectively, of adjoining classes. The upper and lower *class limits* indicate the values included within the class.

When the variable is continuous, with classes of the form, say, '55 – under 60'; '60 – under 65'; etc., the class boundaries are the same as the class limits and can usually be clearly defined. For example with a class of the form '55 – under 60', the class limits are 55 and 60 (the *lower class limit* being 55, the *upper class limit* being 60, and the *class interval* being 5).

When the variable is discrete, with classes of the form, say, '30 – 39'; '40 – 49'; '50 – 59'; etc. we need to distinguish between the class limits and class boundaries, which must be more carefully considered than when dealing with a continuous variable (when, as stated earlier, they are identical).

For example with a class of the form, say, '30 – 39', the class limits are 30 and 39, but for reasons that will become clear later we need to define class boundaries which ensure that there is no gap between adjacent classes (i.e. there is a clear, well–defined, demarcation value). The class boundaries in this case are 29.5 and 39.5, and the class interval equals 10 (i.e. the difference between the class boundaries).

(N.B. The interval '30 – 39' actually contains 10 values of the variable, viz 30, 31, 32, ... 38, 39.)

Likewise, with a class of '40 – 49', we again obtain the class boundaries by reducing the lower class limit by 0.5, and increasing the upper class limit by 0.5. The class boundaries are hence 39.5 and 49.5, and the class interval again equals 10.

A class is said to be 'open–ended' if it is of the form, for example, 'less than 10' or '50 and over' i.e. either the lower limit or the upper limit is absent. By convention the class interval of an open–ended class is taken to be the same as that of the adjacent class. Open–ended classes should generally have low corresponding frequencies

The purpose of grouping is to reduce data that is spread over a large range into a more comprehensive form. The *number of classes* used depends largely on the amount of data to be processed, but as a general guide will usually lie between five and fifteen. Also, the classes must be constructed so that each data value can only lie in ONE class. There should be no ambiguity as to the class in which any particular data value lies.

It should be remembered that when data is presented in the form of a 'grouped frequency distribution' a certain amount of accuracy is lost as the exact data values are no longer displayed.

3.1 Construction of a Grouped Frequency Distribution for a Continuous Variable

Consider the following set of raw data representing the height (in cm) of 28 children.

58.1	63.8	60.8	58.3	57.8	61.4	58.9
60.2	54.3	61.8	61.0	57.2	60.5	59.7
62.2	56.2	59.1	60.3	59.9	65.9	59.2
55.7	58.6	56.8	62.9	61.6	58.5	59.5

To group the above data first pick out the lowest and highest values of the variable. These values are 54.3cm and 65.9cm respectively. We thus need to cover a range of approximately 12cm and, for 28 items, 6 classes of width 2cm suggest themselves as suitable.

Starting with the nearest whole number (54cm) below the lowest data value (54.3cm), the class limits can now be stated. As the variable, height, is a continuous one, these must be written as '54cm and up to but not including 56cm ', or more briefly as ' 54cm and under 56cm '. These classes can then be listed on the frequency table.

Each value of the data is now taken and allocated to its appropriate class. The use of 'tally marks' as shown below facilitates greatly the construction of such frequency tables.

Heights of Children in cm	Tally	Number of Children (frequency)
54 & under 56	//	2
56 & under 58	////	4
58 & under 60	///// /////	10
60 & under 62	///// ///	8
62 & under 64	///	3
64 & under 66	/	1
		——
		28

The frequency column should always be added up to check that no data value has been omitted or counted twice.

It should be noted that alternative values for the 'class interval', 'class limits' etc could have been chosen, but generally speaking these values should be kept as straightforward as possible (allowing for a reasonable number of classes). For example, choosing a 'class interval' of 2.75 cm, say, with the resulting fractional values for the 'class limits' should be avoided.

3.2 Construction of a Grouped Frequency Distribution for a Discrete Variable

Consider the following set of raw data representing the I.Q. of 30 children at a junior school.

90	100	118	89	111	98
71	115	132	93	96	80
98	103	81	95	102	108
107	63	97	84	85	92
93	103	86	105	99	78

The method of construction of the grouped frequency distribution is similar to that used for the case of a continuous variable.

The lowest value = 63

The highest value = 132

The range is 69, and the 30 values suggest the classes given below as being suitable, which, after using 'tally–marks', produces the following grouped frequency distribution.

I.Q.	f
60 – 69	1
70 – 79	2
80 – 89	6
90 – 99	10
100 – 109	7
110 – 119	3
120 and over	1
	—
	30

4. Histogram

Frequency distributions may be represented graphically by means of a special block diagram called a histogram. This is similar to a bar chart without the gaps between the bars. The horizontal scale of a histogram always refers to the variable with the *class boundaries* being marked off along the horizontal scale. The height of the rectangle (i.e. bar) is such that the area of the rectangle is proportional to the frequency in that class.

The height of the rectangle (i.e. bar) on the vertical axis for each class can be scaled directly in frequency (i.e. equated to the frequency of the corresponding class) provided all the class intervals are equal.

4.1 Histogram (Continuous Variable)

Consider the grouped frequency distribution in Section 3.1.

Heights of Children in cm	frequency
54 & under 56	2
56 & under 58	4
58 & under 60	10
60 & under 62	8
62 & under 64	3
64 & under 66	1

The following histogram represents the above grouped frequency distribution (which has equal class intervals).

Diagram 6.1

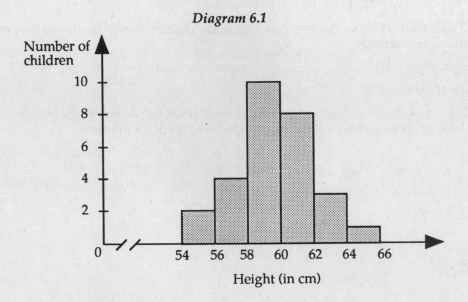

4.2 Histogram (Discrete Variable)

Consider the grouped frequency distribution in section 3.2.

I.Q.	f
60 – 69	1
70 – 79	2
80 – 89	6
90 – 99	10
100 – 109	7
110 – 119	3
120 and over	1
	30

The following histogram represents the above grouped frequency distribution (which has equal class intervals). Note that because we are dealing with a discrete variable, we must identify the class–boundaries which we mark off along the horizontal axis.

Diagram 6.2

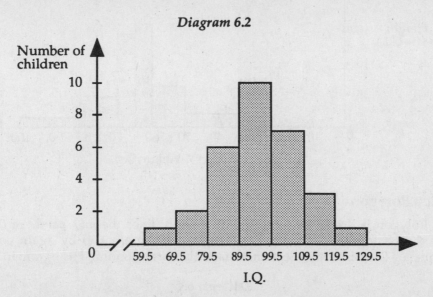

Note that the open–ended class '120 and over' is considered to have the same width as the adjacent class.

4.3 Unequal Class Intervals

The following data, relating to the weight of machine components, have unequal class intervals and so, when drawing a histogram, the height of the rectangle (i.e. bar) for each class no longer equals the frequency corresponding to that class. Instead we need to construct two extra columns, as illustrated below, and the height of the rectangles now ensures that the areas of the rectangles are proportional to the frequency. (See Diagram 6.3)

Weight (Kgs)	f	Class Interval	Height
30 – under 50	40	20	2 (= 40/20)
50 – under 60	64	10	6.4
60 – under 65	80	5	16
65 – under 70	72	5	14.4
70 – under 80	48	10	4.8
80 – under 100	32	20	1.6

where 'Height' $= \dfrac{\text{'Frequency'}}{\text{'Class Interval'}}$

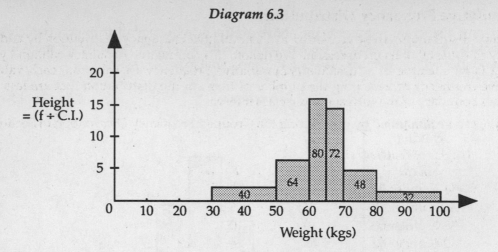

Diagram 6.3

5. Frequency Polygon

A Frequency Polygon is drawn by joining with straight lines the *mid–points* of the tops of the rectangles of the Histogram. This can be illustrated (Diagram 6.4) by again considering the Grouped Frequency Distribution in Section 3.1 (and the corresponding Histogram in Section 4.1).

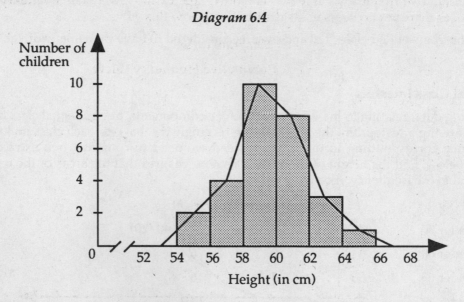

Diagram 6.4

Note particularly that the extremes of the polygon have been taken to the mid–points of the empty classes at each end (these empty classes having the same class interval as their adjacent class) so that the area under the polygon is the same as for the Histogram.

5.1 Frequency Curves

If a Histogram comprises a large number of narrow classes the Frequency Polygon will approximate to a smooth curve, so for simplicity a Frequency Distribution is often represented by a Frequency Curve rather than a Histogram.

6. Cumulative Frequency Distributions

A frequency distribution can be converted to a Cumulative Frequency Distribution by adding each frequency to the total of its predecessors. We denote this cumulative frequency column by 'F'. The following is an example of a 'Less than' Cumulative Frequency Distribution, each value of the cumulative frequency representing the number of items in the distribution that are less than the upper class boundary of the corresponding class interval.

This, again, can be illustrated by considering the Grouped Frequency Distribution in Section 3.1.

Heights of Children in cm	f	F
54 & under 56	2	2
56 & under 58	4	6
58 & under 60	10	16
60 & under 62	8	24
62 & under 64	3	27
64 & under 66	1	28

The cumulative frequency curve (or ogive) is drawn by plotting the cumulative frequency on the vertical axis against the upper class boundary of the corresponding class interval on the horizontal axis. The cumulative frequency value of 0 is plotted against the lower class boundary of the first class interval as there are no items in the distribution below this value.

Diagram 6.5

Cumulative Frequency Curve

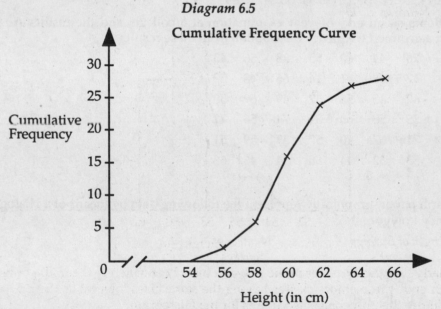

Height (in cm)

It should be remembered that in the case of a grouped frequency distribution for a discrete variable, the *class boundaries* are marked off along the horizontal axis.

6.1 Smoothing Ogives

Though we can join the points of a Cumulative Frequency Curve together with straight lines, in practice the values of the variable are not spread absolutely uniformly over the class interval (as is assumed by joining the points together by straight lines) and smoothing of the straight lines may, in some situations, improve the accuracy of the curve.

Exercises (Answers on page 65)

1. Construct a grouped frequency table from the following data concerning the weekly wages of part–time production workers at a certain factory. Choose the number of classes so that the data can conveniently be covered by classes of £10 width.

22.50	36.82	17.20	42.64	27.41	41.48
14.34	59.72	25.75	69.47	39.09	23.78
55.13	77.60	52.56	34.22	23.98	36.56
48.92	28.46	34.66	47.68	17.74	49.38
31.36	65.21	24.35	45.34	33.48	20.00
31.55	49.12	12.92	53.40	30.64	38.68
21.63	47.88	35.70	38.32	11.23	37.38
44.60	24.64	37.85	27.72	43.25	29.80
40.16	12.45	28.10	58.37	26.08	34.43
19.51	30.30	72.66	35.38	20.70	63.07
61.83	31.92	45.72	23.58	42.83	56.92
36.74	51.42	15.38	41.75	67.62	33.52
30.05	14.86	25.83	50.00	13.57	32.64
22.14	32.86	39.72	26.44	38,84	16.64

2. Fifty students sit an end–of–year examination at a college, and the results are given below. Construct a grouped frequency distribution from these results.

31	76	44	60	55	28	56	43
78	47	68	51	14	66	48	59
32	62	45	53	52	49	69	30
55	35	58	60	31	74	56	22
59	71	67	40	57	39	59	51
38	53	32	44	88	54	46	68
42	57						

3. Using graph paper, graphically represent the following data by means of a Histogram and also a Frequency Polygon.

Length of Springs (in cm)	Number of Springs
1.30 & under 1.35	12
1.35 & under 1.40	34
1.40 & under 1.45	77
1.45 & under 1.50	145
1.50 & under 1.55	182
1.55 & under 1.60	171
1.60 & under 1.65	80
1.65 & under 1.70	39
1.70 & under 1.75	10

4. Draw a histogram to graphically represent the following grouped frequency distribution representing the number of forms checked per day, in an office, over a period of 60 days.

No of forms checked per day	No. of days
65 – 69	3
70 – 74	8
75 – 79	10
80 – 84	15
85 – 89	14
90 – 94	6
95 – 99	3
100 and over	1

5. Draw the Histogram for the following grouped frequency distribution allowing for the classes being of unequal width.

Salesmens' Weekly commission (in £)	Number of Salesmen
Under 12	6
12 & Under 16	10
16 & Under 20	20
20 & Under 24	28
24 & Under 26	28
26 & Under 27	21
27 & Under 28	19
28 & Under 30	20
30 & Under 34	16
34 & Under 40	12

6. The following grouped frequency distribution represents the number of miles travelled per day by a fleet of 70 taxis.

No. of miles	No. of taxis
Under 40	1
40 – under 45	3
45 – under 50	7
50 – under 55	14
55 – under 60	20
60 – under 65	16
65 – under 70	6
70 – under 75	2
75 and over	1

Graphically represent this data by means of:

a) A histogram

b) A Cumulative Frequency Distribution

7. The following Grouped Frequency Distribution represents the number of hours lost due to sickness by employees at a certain factory. Construct a 'less than' Cumulative Frequency Distribution from this data and hence draw the Cumulative Frequency Curve. Graphically estimate:

   a) the number of employees who lost less than 1 week of 44 hours due to sickness.

   b) the least number of hours lost by the most absent half of the employees over the same period.

Number of hours lost	Number of Employees
0 & under 10	23
10 & under 20	29
20 & under 30	43
30 & under 40	31
40 & under 50	23
50 & under 60	14
60 & under 70	11
70 & under 80	4
80 & under 90	2

8. Graphically represent the distribution in Question 4 by means of a 'less than' cumulative frequency curve, and hence estimate the number of days on which:

   a) less than 77 forms were checked;

   b) more than 86 forms were checked.

Short Answers

Questions 1 – 6: Tables/Diagrams

7. Diagram

   a) approx. 135

   b) approx. 28

8. Diagram

   a) approx. 17

   b) approx. 17

7 Measures of Central Tendency

1. Introduction

Measures of 'central tendency' or 'location' refer to values of the variable that are typical of all the observed values of the data. i.e. A value around which the other values are centred. Three measures of central tendency will be considered here:

i) Arithmetic Mean – This is the average of the values in a distribution.

ii) Mode – This is the most frequently occuring value in a distribution.

iii) Median – This is the middle value in a distribution.

Example

The following represent the examination marks of nine students (in percentage terms).

14, 72, 60, 40, 28, 30, 35, 60, 75

i) $\text{Mean} = \dfrac{14 + 72 + 60 + \text{.......} + 60 + 75}{9} = \dfrac{414}{9} = \textbf{46}$

ii) Mode = **60** (this value occurs twice)

iii) If we write these marks in order of magnitude, we have

14, 28, 30, 35, 40, 60, 60, 72, 75

The middle value (i.e. the 5th value) is 40

Median = **40**

2. Arithmetic Mean

The arithmetic mean is the 'average' value of a set of data and is equal to the sum of the observations divided by the number of observations.

The arithmetic mean of a population, referred to as the population mean, is denoted by μ.

The arithmetic mean of a sample, referred to as the sample mean, is denoted by $\bar{x}$ and can be represented by the formula:

$$\bar{x} = \frac{\sum\limits_{i}^{n} x_i}{n}$$

or, in abbreviated form,

$$\bar{x} = \frac{\sum x}{n}$$

where $x_i = i^{th}$ observation and n = number of observations

When the data is in the form of a frequency distribution, the sample mean can be calculated using the formula:

$$\bar{x} = \frac{\sum\limits^{n} f_i x_i}{\sum\limits^{n} f_i}$$

or, in abbreviated form,

$$\bar{x} = \frac{\sum fx}{\sum f}$$

An example of the calculation of the sample mean when the data is in the form of a frequency distribution is given below:

Example

The following data relates to the number of days taken off work by 61 men in a factory over a period of one month.

Days off (x):	0	1	2	3	4	5	6
No. of men (f):	6	8	15	12	9	7	4

The Arithmetic Mean is calculated as follows:

x	f	fx
0	6	0
1	8	8
2	15	30
3	12	36
4	9	36
5	7	35
6	4	24
	61	169

$$\bar{x} = \frac{\sum fx}{\sum f} = \frac{169}{61} = 2.77$$

The average number of days taken off work per month by each man equals **2.77**.

To calculate the arithmetic mean when the data is in the form of a grouped frequency distribution we use the same method as above with the mid–points of the class–intervals being taken as the 'x' values.

Example

The following data relates to the weekly wages of 84 part–time workers at a particular factory. The average weekly wage of employees is calculated as follows:

Weekly wages (in £)	No. of employees f	Mid-point x	fx
10 – under 20	11	15	165
20 – under 30	19	25	475
30 – under 40	25	35	875
40 – under 50	14	45	630
50 – under 60	8	55	440
60 – under 70	5	65	325
70 – under 80	2	75	150
	84		3060

$$\bar{x} = \frac{\Sigma fx}{\Sigma f} = \frac{3060}{84} = 36.43$$

The average weekly wage of the part–time employees is £36.43.

3. Mode

The mode is the observation which occurs most often and need not be unique (i.e. a distribution may have more than one mode).

When dealing with a grouped frequency distribution we are no longer dealing with individual values. In such a case we can identify the *modal class* i.e. the class with the highest frequency. It is then possible to estimate the value of the mode, either by calculation or graphically.

The mode can be graphically estimated from a histogram as illustrated in the following example.

Example

Consider again the example relating to the weekly wages of 84 part–time employees.

Weekly wages (in £)	No. of employees
10 – under 20	11
20 – under 30	19
30 – under 40	25
40 – under 50	14
50 – under 60	8
60 – under 70	5
70 – under 80	2
	84

This distribution can be represented by a histogram as shown in Diagram 7.1.

Diagram 7.1

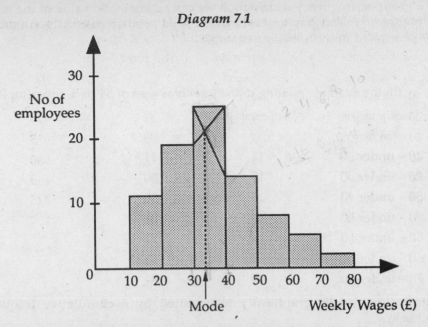

To graphically estimate the mode we first identify the modal class – this is the class containing the modal value (ie the class with the highest rectangle in the histogram). Next we draw crossing lines, as illustrated above, in the rectangle of the modal class. A vertical line is then drawn down from the point of intersection of the crossing lines to the horizontal axis and the point where this vertical line meets the horizontal axis is our estimate of the mode. In the above example our estimate of the mode is approximately £33.

Alternatively, when the data is in the form of a grouped frequency distribution, the mode can be estimated using the following formula:

$$\text{Mode} = L + \left[\frac{f_1 - f_0}{2f_1 - f_0 - f_2}\right]c$$

where   L is the lower bound of the modal class

       c is the class interval of the modal class

       f_0 is the frequency of the class before the modal class

       f_1 is the frequency of the modal class

       f_2 is the frequency of the class after the modal class

4. Median

If we were to list all the values of a distribution in order of magnitude, then the median would be the middle value. Should there be an even number of values in the distribution then none of them represents the position where half of the distribution is above and half below. In this case the value of the median is taken as the average of the two middle values.

When dealing with a grouped frequency distribution, the median is defined as that value which divides the frequency distribution into two equal halves. If we recall that in a histogram the areas of the rectangles are proportional to the frequencies, then we can say that a vertical line drawn through the median divides the histogram into two parts of equal area.

In the case of a grouped frequency distribution we can estimate the value of the median either by calculation or graphically. The graphical estimation of the median (using the cumulative frequency distribution) is illustrated in the following example.

Example

Consider again the example relating to the weekly wages of 84 part–time employees.

Weekly wages (in £)	No. of employees	F
10 – under 20	11	11
20 – under 30	19	30
30 – under 40	25	55
40 – under 50	14	69
50 – under 60	8	77
60 – under 70	5	82
70 – under 80	2	84

This distribution can be graphically represented by a cumulative frequency curve as illustrated below.

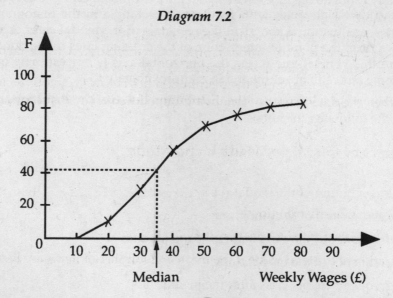

Diagram 7.2

To graphically estimate the median we first divide the total frequency in half (i.e. in this case 84/2 = 42) and from this point on the vertical axis we draw a horizontal line across to the curve. At the point where this horizontal line meets the curve we draw a vertical line down to the horizontal axis, and the point where this vertical line meets the horizontal axis is our estimate of the median (as illustrated above). In this case our estimate of the median is £34.80.

We thus conclude that 42 of the part–time employees earn less than £34.80 and 42 of them earn more than £34.80.

Alternatively, the median may be calculated using the following formula.

$$\text{Median} = L + \left[\frac{\frac{n}{2} - F_{m-1}}{f_m} \right] c$$

where
L = Lower bound of the median class

c = Class interval of the median class

n = Total frequency

f_m = frequency of the median class

F_{m-1} = cumulative frequency of the class before the median class.

N.B. The median class is the class containing the median value of the distribution. In the above example we can see from examining the cumulative frequency column that the $\frac{n}{2}$th value (i.e. the 42nd value) lies in the class '30 – under 40'. This is therefore the median class.

4.1 Quartiles

There are two quartiles which are denoted by Q_1 and Q_3.

The two quartiles together with the median divide the distribution into four quarters. Thus if we were to list all the values of a distribution in order of magnitude, then the median is the middle value (and is equivalent to Q_2); the lower quartile, Q_1, is the value above which three quarters of the distribution lies, (i.e. one quarter of the distribution lies below Q_1); and the upper quartile, Q_3, is the value above which one quarter of the distribution lies. (i.e. three quarters of the distribution lies below Q_3).

5. Characteristics of the Mean, Median and Mode

The Mean

1. Uses every value in the distribution.

2. Can be used for further mathematical processing.

3. Allows calculation of the total value if the mean and number of items are known.

$$n\overline{x} = \sum_{i}^{n} x_i$$

4. Is influenced by a few exceptionally high or low values in a distribution.

The Median

1. Uses only one or two values in the distribution.

2. Cannot be used for further mathematical processing

3. Does not allow calculation of the total value of items.

4. Is not affected by extreme values, or by incomplete data values providing 'n' is known

The Mode

1. Is the value which occurs most often or about which the other values are most concentrated.

2. Is not suitable for further mathematical processing.

3. Does not allow calculation of the total value of items.

4. Is not affected by incomplete data or extreme values.

5. Can occur more than once in a distribution though this usually means that the data are really more than one distinct distribution superimposed.

When a frequency distribution is perfectly symmetrical, then the Mean, Median and Mode have the same value. When a distribution is not symmetrical, its Mean, being affected by the more extreme values, shifts towards the more extended side. The Median shifts in the same direction but not so far as the Mean, while the Mode stays at the position where the data values are most concentrated.

Diagram 7.3

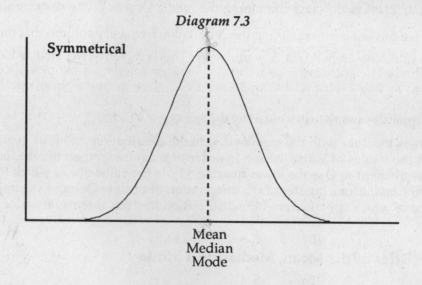

Diagram 7.4

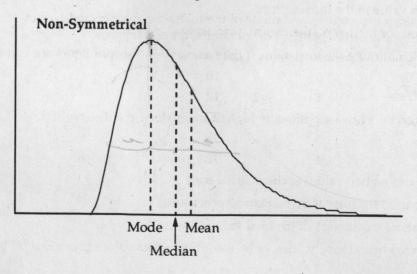

Exercises (Answers on page 75)

1.   Calculate the mean, median and mode of the following set of data:

   2, 1, 3, 7, 2, 1, 6, 8, 4, 3, 9, 2, 4, 6, 5.

2.   Calculate the mean, median and mode of the following set of data:

   22, 24, 26, 21, 28, 22, 24, 28, 24, 21, 23, 22

3.   a)   The Mean of the following set of numbers is 5 and the Mode is 4. What values have x and y? What is the Median?

   3, 7, x, 9, 4, 2, y

   b)   In 14 consecutive weeks a salesman's commissions in £'s were:

   25, 17, 48, 21, 30, 94, 98, 0, 5, 120, 73, 60, 184, 13

   Find his mean weekly commission.

   If in the next eight weeks his mean commission for the whole period of 22 weeks was reduced by £4.20, what was his mean commission for the last eight weeks?

4.   Calculate the mean, median and mode of the following frequency distribution:

x	f
100	2
101	5
102	12
103	10
104	8
105	5
106	5
107	2

5.   Calculate the mean median and mode of the following frequency distribution representing the number of typing errors per page on a manuscript of 100 pages.

Errors per page	No. of pages
0	10
1	12
2	22
3	19
4	10
5	8
6	10
7	6
8	2
9	1

6. Find the Mean, Median and Mode of the following grouped frequency distribution showing the numbers of savings certificates held by the 800 members of a certain savings group.

Number of Certificates	Number of Members
1 to 100	15
101 to 150	30
151 to 200	60
201 to 250	100
251 to 300	140
301 to 350	240
351 to 400	180
401 to 500	35

7. The recovery time of an aircraft is the time which elapses between its arrival at an airport and it being ready to take off again.

Find the mean, median and modal recovery times for the 100 aircraft shown in the following distribution.

Time (minutes)	Number of Aircraft
5 & under 10	4
10 & under 15	22
15 & under 20	28
20 & under 25	18
25 & under 30	12
30 & under 35	9
35 & under 40	4
40 & under 45	3

8 Measures of

wages of 84 part–time employees (see unit

nployees	F
	11
	30
	55
	69
	77
	82
	84

1. Introduction

Measures of variation provide us with a sin
dispersion of the data, i.e. whether the data are

Three measures of variation will be considered

i) Range

ii) Quartile deviation

iii) Standard Deviation.

2. Range

The range is defined as the difference between means of a cumulative frequency curve as

> *Example*
>
> The following data represents the weekly 8.1
>
> 80, 120, 110, 112, 85, 122, 132, 85,
>
> The range of the employees' pay is given
>
> Range = 132 – 75 = **£57**

The range is an easily understood measure of
disadvantage is that it is greatly influenced by
low values).

3. Quartile Deviation

The Quartile Deviation can be defined as the
median. That is:

$$\text{Quartile Deviation} = \quad \text{60} \quad \text{70} \quad \text{80} \quad \text{90}$$

Weekly Wages (£)

Where M = median

Q_1 = lower (or first) quartile

Q_3 = upper (or third) quartile

The expression ($Q_3 - Q_1$) is often referred to a
of the data (when the data are arranged in ord

The quartile deviation is given by

$$\text{Quartile deviation} = \frac{Q_3 - Q_1}{2} = \frac{20.45}{2} = £10.225$$

Unlike the range, the quartile deviation is not greatly influenced by extreme values of the data.

4. Standard Deviation

The standard deviation measures the spread of the data about the arithmetic mean. The greater the difference between the individual data items and the mean the greater will be the standard deviation.

The standard deviation of a population is denoted by the Greek letter σ, and the standard deviation of a sample is denoted by s. The square of the standard deviation is referred to as the variance.

The standard deviation is both the most common and the most important measure of variation. This is mainly due to its mathematical properties which make it suitable for further mathematical processing e.g. frequent use is made of the standard deviation in statistical estimation and testing.

4.1 Standard Deviation of Ungrouped Data

The standard deviation of a sample of ungrouped data can be calculated using the following formula:

$$s = \sqrt{\frac{\sum_{i}^{n}(x_i - \bar{x})^2}{n}} = \sqrt{\frac{\sum_{i}^{n}x_i^2}{n} - \bar{x}^2} = \sqrt{\frac{\sum x^2}{n} - \bar{x}^2} \text{ (in abbreviated form)}$$

where   n = size of the sample

$\bar{x}$ = sample mean

x_i = ith observation

N.B. If the sample standard deviation is to be used as an estimate of the population standard deviation then it can be shown that a better estimate is obtained if we use the formula:

$$s = \sqrt{\frac{\sum_{i}^{n}(x_i - \bar{x})^2}{n-1}}$$

Example

Calculate the standard deviation of the following set of data:

19, 22, 23, 25, 27, 28.

x	x^2
19	361
22	484
23	529
25	625
27	729
28	784
144	3512

78

$\Sigma x = 144; \quad \Sigma x^2 = 3512$

$$\bar{x} = \frac{\Sigma x}{n} = \frac{144}{6} = 24$$

$$s = \sqrt{\frac{\Sigma x^2}{n} - \bar{x}^2} \quad \text{(in abbreviated form)}$$

$$= \sqrt{9.33}$$

$$= 3.06$$

4.2 Standard Deviation of a Frequency Distribution

When the data is expressed in the form of a frequency distribution the sample standard deviation can be calculated using the following formula:

$$s = \sqrt{\frac{\sum\limits^{n} f_i(x_i - \bar{x})^2}{\sum\limits^{n} f_i}} = \sqrt{\frac{\sum\limits^{n} f_i x_i^2}{\sum\limits^{n} f_i} - \bar{x}^2} = \sqrt{\frac{\Sigma f x^2}{\Sigma f} - \bar{x}^2} \quad \text{(in abbreviated form)}$$

where $\Sigma f = n =$ size of the sample (i.e. total frequency)

$\bar{x} =$ sample mean

$x_i = i^{\text{th}}$ observation

Example

Calculate the standard deviation of the following frequency distribution:

x:	1	2	3	4	5	6
f:	2	6	8	12	8	4

x	f	fx	fx^2
1	2	2	2
2	6	12	24
3	8	24	72
4	12	48	192
5	8	40	200
6	4	24	144
	40	150	634

$\Sigma f = 40; \quad \Sigma fx = 150; \quad \Sigma fx^2 = 634$

$$\bar{x} = \frac{\Sigma fx}{\Sigma f} = \frac{150}{40} = 3.75$$

$$s = \sqrt{\frac{\Sigma f x^2}{\Sigma f} - \bar{x}^2} = \sqrt{\frac{634}{40} - 3.75^2}$$

$$s = \sqrt{\frac{\Sigma f x^2}{\Sigma f} - \overline{x}^2} = \sqrt{\frac{634}{40} - 3.75^2}$$

$$= \sqrt{1.7875}$$

$$= 1.34$$

4.3 Standard Deviation of a Grouped Frequency Distribution

To calculate the standard deviation of a grouped frequency distribution we use the same method as illustrated in the above example with the mid–points of the class intervals being taken as the 'x' values. This is the case whether or not the variable under consideration is continuous or discrete, and also whether or not the class intervals are equal.

Example

Consider again the example relating to the weekly wages of 84 part–time employees (see unit on Measures of Central Tendency – Section 2).

Calculate the standard deviation of this distribution.

Weekly wages (in £)	No. of employees f	Mid-point x	fx	fx^2
10 – under 20	11	15	165	2475
20 – under 30	19	25	475	11875
30 – under 40	25	35	875	30625
40 – under 50	14	45	630	28350
50 – under 60	8	55	440	24200
60 – under 70	5	65	325	21125
70 – under 80	2	75	150	11250
	84		3060	129900

$$\overline{x} = \frac{\Sigma f x}{\Sigma f} = \frac{3060}{84} = 36.43$$

$$s = \sqrt{\frac{\Sigma f x^2}{\Sigma f} - \overline{x}^2} = \sqrt{1546.63 - 1327.04}$$

$$= \sqrt{219.39}$$

$$= £14.81$$

5. Skewness

When a histogram or a frequency curve derived from a frequency distribution is perfectly symmetrical, the distribution is said to have zero skewness. In this case it can also be noted that the mean equals the median equals the mode.

When a histogram or a frequency curve is not symmetrical, and the mean and median move away from the mode, the distribution is said to be skewed.

When the shape of the distribution is extended towards the larger positive values of the variable, the distribution is said to be positively skewed. When the shape of the distribution is extended towards the smaller or negative values of the variable, the distribution is said to be negatively skewed.

Diagram 8.2

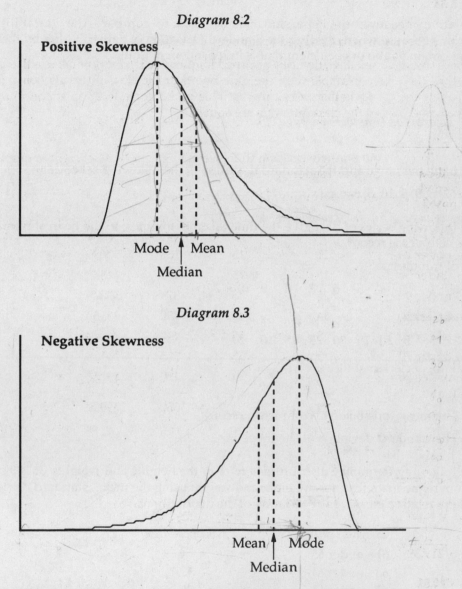

Positive Skewness

Mode ↑ Mean

Median

Diagram 8.3

Negative Skewness

Mean ↑ Mode

Median

One measure of skewness is 'Pearson's' Coefficient of Skewness which is given by

$$\frac{\text{Mean} - \text{Mode}}{\text{Standard Deviation}}$$

The larger this coefficient, the more skew the distribution. The sign of this coefficient tells us the direction of the skewness.

If the distribution is perfectly symmetrical then this coefficient equals zero.

6. Coefficient of Variation

The coefficient of variation is a relative measure of dispersion based on the Mean and Standard Deviation of a distribution. The coefficient of variation is given by

$$\frac{\text{Standard Deviation}}{\text{Mean}} \times 100$$

Such relative measures of dispersion can be used to compare the variability of different distributions because when dividing the Standard Deviation of a distribution by the corresponding Mean, we obtain a ratio or coefficient that is independent of units.

 Exercises (Answers on page 89)

1. Calculate the range and the standard deviation of the following set of data:

    7, 12, 3, 5, 9, 6, 10, 5, 6

2. The following series of data give the time taken in minutes, to the nearest minute, by clerks to complete a case record.

    No. of minutes:

       1   2   3   4   5   6   7   8   9 10

    No. of clerks:

       2   3   5 10 15 30 25 15 10 5

    Total no. of clerks = 120

    Calculate:

    a) The mean time taken to complete a record.

    b) The standard deviation of the time.

3. The following frequency distributions refer to the heights and weights of 100 school children. Compare the main features of height and weight using the mean, standard deviation, the mode and the relative measures of variation of the distributions.

Heights (cm)	No. of children
61 - under 63	4
63 - under 65	12
65 - under 67	27
67 - under 69	32
69 - under 71	16
71 - under 73	6
73 - under 75	3

Weight (in units of ¼ Kg.)	No. of children
100 - under 110	7
110 - under 120	12
120 - under 130	20
130 - under 140	25
140 - under 150	20
150 - under 160	6
160 - under 170	5
170 - under 180	2
180 - under 190	1
190 - under 200	1
200 - under 210	1

4. A company making electronic components is testing the performance of a new machine. The number of components produced by this machine was noted at the end of each day for 120 days. The information obtained is given in the following table.

Number of components produced per day	Number of days
110 - 119	2
120 - 129	4
130 - 139	14
140 - 149	29
150 - 159	23
160 - 169	22
170 - 179	12
180 - 189	8
190 - 199	4
200 - 209	2

i) Illustrate the given information by

   a) a Histogram

   b) a Cumulative Frequency Curve

ii) Calculate the mean number of components produced per day and the standard deviation for this distribution.

iii) Graphically estimate the median of this distribution.

iv) Find the number of days on which less than 135 components were produced. On 10% of the days the number of components produced was less than N, find the value of N.

5. A large store makes periodic checks on the value of stock held. 250 items were selected at random and their values were noted. The table below gives the results obtained.

Value of item (£)	No. of items
Under 10	2
10 - under 20	6
20 - under 30	8
30 - under 40	15
40 - under 50	42
50 - under 60	68
60 - under 70	49
70 - under 80	25
80 - under 90	18
90 - under 100	12
100 - under 110	4
110 - under 120	1

a) Calculate the mean and standard deviation of this distribution.

b) Graphically estimate the median value of this distribution and also the Quartile Deviation.

c) Estimate the value of the whole of the stock if it is known to consist of 3426 items.

6. In an investigation of road usage, the number of vehicles crossing an electronic counter in each 24 hour period was recorded for 120 days. The results are given in the following table.

Number of vehicles per 24 hours	Number of days these nos of vehicles passed
Under 500	2
500 and under 550	6
550 and under 600	9
600 and under 650	20
650 and under 700	25
700 and under 750	23
750 and under 800	16
800 and under 850	12
850 and under 900	5
900 and over	2

a) Draw the histogram of these data.

b) From the histogram estimate the Mode graphically.

c) Calculate the Arithmetic Mean, the Median and the Standard Deviation of these data.

d) Compare and contrast the Mean, Median and Mode.

7. The following table gives the amounts of bonus earned by the sales representatives of a certain company in a particular week.

Amount of Bonus (in £'s)	No. of Representatives
1 and under 3	10
3 and under 5	16
5 and under 7	11
7 and under 9	5
9 and under 11	4
11 and under 13	2
13 and under 15	1
15 and over	1

a) Calculate the arithmetic mean and the standard deviation of the amount of bonus.

b) How much money would the firm have to provide in order to pay the bonus?

c) What percentage of the sales representatives would receive less than £10 bonus? (You may find this graphically or by calculation).

8. A firm which employs 100 men intends to introduce a bonus scheme enabling employees to earn up to £40 per week on top of their basic wage. Details of the employees' bonus earnings from a pilot run of this scheme are given in the following table.

Weekly Bonus (in £'s)	No. of Employees
0 - under 4	9
4 - under 8	10
8 - under 12	12
12 - under 16	12
16 - under 20	15
20 - under 24	14
24 - under 28	10
28 - under 32	7
32 - under 36	6
36 - under 40	5
	100

a) Calculate the mean weekly bonus earned and also the standard deviation.

b) Draw a 'less than' Cumulative Frequency Curve of the distribution.

c) From the Cumulative Frequency Curve estimate

   i) The median of the distribution

   ii) The percentage of employees earning less than £33.50 bonus.

   iii) The percentage of employees earning more than £13 bonus.

9. A small supermarket operates one check-out point with a cashier. Customers are checked out one at a time on a first come first served basis. Check-out times vary depending upon the number of items bought.

The following data relate to the first fifteen customers checked out one morning.

Customer	Arrival time at check-out point	Check-out completion time
1	9.05 a.m.	9.08 a.m.
2	9.09	9.14
3	9.14	9.15
4	9.17	9.19
5	9.20	9.22
6	9.25	9.31
7	9.31	9.35
8	9.36	9.38
9	9.38	9.40
10	9.41	9.44
11	9.44	9.48
12	9.48	9.50
13	9.50	9.53
14	9.53	9.58
15	10.01	10.05

a) In order to illustrate the variability in the above data, find the check-out time for each customer and hence construct a frequency distribution for the check-out times of customers.

b) From the distribution derived in part (a) calculate

i) The mean check-out time per customer

ii) The standard deviation of the check-out time.

iii) The modal check-out time.

iv) The median check-out time.

10. The following histogram represents the size of petrol purchases by a sample of 100 customers at a particular service station under normal working conditions.

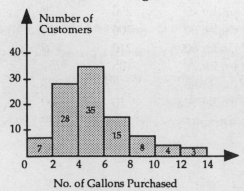

No. of Gallons Purchased

a) From this histogram estimate the value of the Mode.

b) Calculate the Mean and Standard Deviation of the sample.

c) Draw a Cumulative Frequency Distribution to represent the data given in the histogram and hence estimate the median, quartiles and quartile deviation.

d) Interpret the meaning of the measures of central tendency and spread that you have calculated.

11. In a bakery a large number of cakes were weighed and the following weights recorded:

Weights (grams)	No. of Cakes
Under 54	12
54 and under 56	44
56 and under 58	168
58 and under 60	352
60 and under 62	448
62 and under 64	344
64 and under 66	176
66 and under 68	48
68 and over	8

a) Calculate the mean weight of the cakes and the corresponding standard deviation.

b) Estimate graphically the percentage of cakes weighing less than the weight represented by 'two standard deviations below the mean weight'. Comment on the percentage you find.

12. The management of WEARMORE SUPERCLOTHING have noticed that some stores in their chain have been more successful than others in terms of total turnover and profit. It has been suggested that - although all stores in the chain stock the same goods and experience the same degree of competition from other clothing shops - perhaps the location and the nature of the goods offered ('upmarket' and 'downmarket') may influence total turnover.

In order to assess whether this is so, the management have conducted a survey of customer expenditure in two stores of contrasting location. Store A is situated in the inner city and Store B is situated in a suburb. Part of the results of the survey are given below:

Customer Expenditure (£)	No of Customers Store A	Store B
10 and under 20	40	5
20 and under 30	120	10
30 and under 40	200	20
40 and under 50	300	40
50 and under 60	210	100
60 and under 70	100	250
70 and under 80	20	275
80 and under 90	10	200
90 or more	0	100
	1000	1000

You are required to write a report, advising the management on the difference and similarities in the pattern of customer expenditure in Stores A and B. Include in your report specific consideration of:

i) The frequency distributions as represented by frequency polygons drawn on the same axes.

ii) The average customer expenditure in each store.

iii) The variability of customer expenditure.

iv) Advice to the management on whether each store should allocate more or less floorspace to upmarket or downmarket goods. Justify your advice.

13. Histagon Computers Limited are considering placing an order for components from either Company A or Company B. The life of this particular component is critical. To help them decide, Histagon tested 100 components from each company and noted the life (in hours) of each component. These are as follows:

Time (in hrs)	No of components	
	Company A	Company B
50 - under 60	6	3
60 - under 70	13	4
70 - under 80	25	10
80 - under 90	14	18
90 - under 100	11	19
100 - under 110	9	24
110 - under 120	7	10
120 - under 130	6	5
130 - under 140	6	7
140 - under 150	3	0

i) Draw a frequency polygon for each company on the same graph. Find the mean time for each company.

ii) Find the median and quartile deviation for each company by graph or otherwise.

iii) Using the results from parts (i) and (ii) write a report advising Histagon which company to place an order with.

Short Answers

1. 9, 2.66

2. 6.275, 1.923

3. Height: 67.48, 2.617, 3.88
    Weight: 135.8, 19.009, 14

4. ii) 156.083, 18.394
    iii) 154
    iv) 135

5. a) 58.88, 19.198
    b) 58, 11
    c) £201722.88

6. b) 685
    c) 698.75, 696, 95.73

7. a) 5.68, 3.28
    b) £284
    c) 63%

8. a) 18.08, 10.056
    c) £17.8, 92%, 66%

9. b) 3.2, 1.38, 2, 3

10. a) 4.52
    b) 5.26, 2.72
    c) 4.86, 3.29, 6.67, 1.69

11. a) 61.005, 2.84
    b) 2.625%

12. ii) Store A: 44.5, Store B: 71.7
    iii) Store A: 14.1, Store B: 15

13. i) A: 90.3, B: 97.5
    ii) A: 85, 17 B: 99, 12

9 Probability

1. Introduction

Probability theory has a wide range of applications in business, including decision making and the assessment of risk, and it forms the basis of the whole area of statistical testing. This chapter considers the basic concepts of probability.

Probability is concerned with future occurrences. Consider an experiment which consists of a number of *trials*, each trial being a process which generates a particular *outcome* (ie result). We can refer to each outcome, or any set of outcomes, as an *event*. The probability that an event will occur always takes a value between 0 and 1 inclusive; this can be represented symbolically as

$$0 \le P(E) \le 1$$

where   E   = some future event (that may or may not happen)

and $P(E)$ = the Probability that the event E will occur

We can extend this notation to define E as the non–occurrence of the event $\bar{E}$.

Example

Consider, as an experiment, the rolling of a die. Each time the die is rolled can be considered as a *trial*. There are six possible *outcomes* to each trial (ie the numbers 1,2,3....6).

We could then, for example, define the event E as follows:

E: Obtaining a number greater then 4

We can then define $\bar{E}$ as:

$\bar{E}$: Not obtaining a number greater than 4.

It should be noted that:

$P(E) = 1$ if and only if the event E is certain to happen (i.e. as certain as any future event can be).

$P(E) = 0$ if and only if the event E is certain not to happen.

If two events cannot both occur at the same time. they are said to be *mutually exclusive*.

If the occurrence or non–occurrence of an event in no way effects the occurrence of another event, then the two events are said to be *independent*.

2. Approaches to Probability

There are three approaches to the numerical evaluation of probabilities.

The Statistical Approach

The Subjective Approach

The Analytical Approach

2.1 The Statistical Approach

This approach to the evaluation of probabilities depends upon the use of historical data, and is sometimes referred to as the relative frequency approach. It is best illustrated by an example.

Example

The following data relates to the sales of cars per week over a period of 50 weeks at a small garage

No. of cars sold	0	1	2	3	4	5
No. of weeks	12	14	8	6	6	4

From this data we can estimate the probability (i.e. calculate the relative frequency) that in a certain week a particular number of cars are sold.

Let X = No. of cars sold per week

x	f	Relative frequency
0	12	$12/50 = 0.24$
1	14	$14/50 = 0.28$
2	8	0.16
3	6	0.12
4	6	0.12
5	4	0.08
	50	1

The relative frequency is calculated by dividing each individual value of the frequency by the total frequency. The relative frequencies provide us with our estimates of the probability associated with each value of x. Hence we can say that on the basis of our sample of 50 weeks, we estimate that the probability of selling no cars in a particular week at the garage in question is 0.24; the probability of selling two cars in a particular week is 0.16; etc.

2.2 The Subjective Approach

Many situations arise where we may wish to evaluate the probabilities of future events but where we cannot repeat the experiment and thus have no historical data.

An example of this might be a capital investment project involving the investment of, say, £250,000. It would be desirable to have probabilities associated with the events, say:

E_1: The Project will make a profit

E_2: The Project will break even

E_3: The Project will make a loss.

Estimates of such probabilities can be obtained by subjective assessment, taking into account all available information. The problem with such estimates is that they are based upon opinion, and thus upon the person making the estimate. However, the alternative may be to have no such estimates.

2.3 The Analytical Approach

This approach involves the mathematical calculation of probabilities, and these probabilities can be determined before the experiment takes place.

The probability that the event E will occur is given by:

$$P(E) = \frac{\text{Number of favourable outcomes}}{\text{Total number of possible outcomes}}$$

Examples

1. Consider the experiment of drawing one card from a pack.

   a) The probability this card is a king is $^4/_{52}$

   (because there are 4 Kings in a pack of 52 cards).

   b) The probability this card is a club is $^{13}/_{52}$

   (because there are 13 Clubs in a pack of 52 cards).

2. One disc is drawn from a box containing 5 blue discs and 4 red discs.

   The probability that the disc drawn is red is $^4/_9$.

3. Two dice are thrown. Find the probability that the total score equals

   a) Two

   b) Six.

   The list of all possible outcomes are given below:

(1, 1)	(1, 2)	(1, 3)	(1, 4)	(1, 5)	(1, 6)
(2, 1)	(2, 2)	(2, 3)	(2, 4)	(2, 5)	(2, 6)
(3, 1)	(3, 2)	(3, 3)	(3, 4)	(3, 5)	(3, 6)
(4, 1)	(4, 2)	(4, 3)	(4, 4)	(4, 5)	(4, 6)
(5, 1)	(5, 2)	(5, 3)	(5, 4)	(5, 5)	(5, 6)
(6, 1)	(6, 2)	(6, 3)	(6, 4)	(6, 5)	(6, 6)

   a) Probability that the total score equals two is $^1/_{36}$

   N.B. a total score of 'two' can only be obtained by one outcome - (1,1)

   b) Probability that the total score equals six is $^5/_{36}$

   N.B. a total score of 'six' can be obtained by any one of five outcomes - (1,5), (2,4), (3,3), (4,2), (5,1)

The analytical approach is the one that we will be concentrating on in this unit.

3. The Probability of the Non- Occurrence of an Event

If the probability that an event E will occur is given by P(E), then the probability that the event will not occur is given by $P(\bar{E})$ and, because it is certain that either the event E will or will not occur, we can say that:

$$P(E) + P(\bar{E}) = 1$$

Example

Consider drawing a card from a pack. If the event E is defined as:

E: the card drawn is an Ace

then

$\bar{E}$: the card drawn is not an Ace

hence $P(E) = {}^4/_{52}$ and $P(\bar{E}) = {}^{48}/_{52}$

4. The Addition Law of Probability

This is given by

$$P(A + B) = P(A) + P(B) - P(AB)$$

where $P(A + B)$ =The Probability that event A *or* event B occurs

(i.e. at least one of events A, B occur).

$P(AB)$ = The probability that both event A *and* event B occur.

Example

A card is drawn randomly from a pack. Calculate the probability that the card drawn is

i) An Ace or a King

ii) An Ace or a Club

Let us first define

E_1: the card drawn is an Ace

E_2: the card drawn is a King

E_3: the card drawn is a Club

i) We require $P(E_1 + E_2)$

$$P(E_1 + E_2) = P(E_1) + P(E_2) - P(E_1 E_2)$$
$$= {}^4/_{52} + {}^4/_{52} - 0$$
$$= {}^8/_{52}$$

ii) We require $P(E_1 + E_3)$

$$P(E_1 + E_3) = P(E_1) + P(E_3) - P(E_1 E_3)$$
$$= {}^4/_{52} + {}^{13}/_{52} - {}^1/_{52}$$
$$= {}^{16}/_{52}$$

Note that in (i) above, $P(E_1 E_2) = 0$. That is, events E_1 and E_2 are *mutually exclusive*.

More generally, if two events A and B are mutually exclusive then the Addition law reduces to

$$P(A + B) = P(A) + P(B)$$

This rule can be extended to any number of mutually exclusive events

i.e. $P(A + B + C + D + ...) = P(A) + P(B) + P(C) + P(D) + ...$

We should note that if all possible mutually exclusive events are included, one of these is certain to occur, so that the sum of the probabilities of all of these events must equal 1.

Example

Consider, as an experiment, the rolling of a die. The following is a list of all the possible mutually exclusive outcomes.

E_1: The score obtained is 1

E_2: The score obtained is 2

E_3: The score obtained is 3

E_4: The score obtained is 4

E_5: The score obtained is 5

E_6: The score obtained is 6

then

$$P(E_1 + E_2 + E_3 + E_4 + E_5 + E_6) = P(E_1) + P(E_2) + P(E_3) + P(E_4) + P(E_5) + P(E_6) = 1$$

Example

A box contains 10 discs numbered one to ten. Find the probability that a disc, drawn randomly from the box, has an odd number or a number greater than seven.

Let us define the following events:

A: Number on disc is odd

B: Number on disc is greater than seven.

$$P(A) = {}^5/_{10} \qquad P(B) = {}^3/_{10} \qquad P(AB) = {}^1/_{10}$$

$$\therefore P(A + B) = P(A) + P(B) - P(AB)$$
$$= {}^5/_{10} + {}^3/_{10} - {}^1/_{10}$$
$$= {}^7/_{10}$$

5. The Multiplication Law

This is given by:

$$P(AB) = P(A) \times P(B/A)$$

where   P(AB) = The Probability that both event A and event B occur

P(B/A) = The Probability that event B will occur given that event A has already occurred – this is called *Conditional Probability*.

Two or more events are said to be *independent* if the occurrence or non–occurrence of any one of them in no way affects the occurrence of the others.

In particular, if two or more events A, B,… are independent, then the multiplication law reduces to:

$$P(AB) = P(A) \times P(B) \times \dots$$

Example

A coin is flipped twice. Calculate the probability of obtaining two heads

We first define the events of interest as follows:

A: Head obtained on first throw

B: Head obtained on second throw

We require P(AB). Since events A and B are independent we have:

P(AB) $= P(A) \times P(B)$

$\quad = {}^1\!/_2 \times {}^1\!/_2$

$\quad = {}^1\!/_4$

Example

If a coin is flipped and a die is thrown, calculate the probability of obtaining a head *and* a six.

We first define the events of interest as follows:

A: Head is obtained when coin is flipped

B: Six is obtained when die is thrown

Events A and B are clearly independent and we require P(AB). Therefore we have:

P(AB) $= P(A) \times P(B)$

$\quad = {}^1\!/_2 \times {}^1\!/_6$

$\quad = {}^1\!/_{12}$

Example

A box contains 4 blue discs, 5 red discs and one black disc. Two discs are drawn from the box, one after the other (without replacement). Find the probability that both discs are blue.

We first define the events of interest as follows:

A: First disc drawn is blue

B: Second disc drawn is blue

We require P(AB), where events A and B are not independent (i.e. they are dependent). Therefore we have:

P(AB) $= P(A) \times P(B/A)$

$\quad = {}^4\!/_{10} \times {}^3\!/_9$

$\quad = {}^2\!/_{15}$

Note that P(B/A) is the probability that event B occurs given that event A has already occurred. In this example, if event A has already occurred then the number of discs left in the box is 9 of which only 3 are blue. Hence P(B/A) = ${}^3\!/_9$.

Example

Two cards are drawn, consecutively, from a pack. Calculate the probability that the first one is a heart and the second one a club.

We have:

A: First card drawn is a heart

B: Second card drawn is a club

We require P(AB) where events A and B are dependent. Therefore we have:

P(AB) $\quad = P(A) \times P(B/A)$

$\quad = {}^{13}\!/_{52} \times {}^{13}\!/_{51}$

$\quad = {}^{13}\!/_{204}$

6. More Examples

An aircraft engine has a probability of failure of 0.01 (independently of other engines) Aircraft can make a satisfactory landing if at least half of their engines function. What is the probability of

a) A two–engine aircraft crashing due to engine failure

b) A four–engine aircraft crashing due to engine failure.

a) A two–engine aircraft will land safely if at least half of the engines function, so it will only crash if both engines fail. We can first define the following events:

A: Engine number one fails

B: Engine number two fails

We require the probability that both engines fail, which is given by P(AB).

Because events A and B are independent, we have

$P(AB) = P(A) \times P(B) = 0.01 \times 0.01 = \mathbf{0.0001}$

b) A four engined aircraft will land safely if at least half of the engines function, so it will only crash if three or all four engines fail. We can first define the following events:

A: Engine number one fails.

B: Engine number two fails.

C: Engine number three fails.

D: Engine number four fails.

We require:

P(crash) = P(4 engines fail) + P(3 engines fail)

Now:

$$P(4 \text{ engines fail}) = P(ABCD)$$
$$= P(A)\ P(B)\ P(C)\ P(D)$$
$$= (0.01)^4 = 0.00000001$$

Also:

$$P(3 \text{ engines fail}) = P(ABC\bar{D}) + P(AB\bar{C}D) + P(A\bar{B}CD) + P(\bar{A}BCD)$$
$$= 4(0.01)^3(0.99)$$
$$= 0.00000396$$

Therefore, we have:

$$P(\text{crash}) = (0.01)^4 + 0.00000396$$
$$= \mathbf{0.00000397}$$

Exercises (Answers on page 101)

A. Basic Evaluations

1. What are the probabilities of drawing the following cards from a full pack of 52 cards?

   a) A black king

   b) A Court (Picture) card

   c) No card from 2 to 9

   d) A diamond

2. During the last 12 weeks a train, which runs from Monday to Friday, was late on 42 occasions, exactly on time on 12 occasions, early on 4 occasions, and twice did not run. From this information estimate the probability that tomorrow

   a) It will be late

   b) It will not be on time

   c) It will run.

B. Rules of Addition

3. Which of the following events are mutually exclusive?

   a) Rolling a '7' and an '8' with one roll of a *pair* of dice.

   b) Living in Brighton and working in London.

   c) Being a physician and being a college professor.

   d) Drawing an ace and drawing a red card from a pack of cards when one card is drawn.

   e) Getting 2 heads and getting 3 heads in 5 tosses of a coin.

4. What is the probability that on a certain day Smith drives his own car to work, if the probability that he walks to work is 0.15 and the probability that he takes a bus is 0.2? (Assume that there are no other alternatives).

5. In a certain lottery, the probability of drawing a number divisible by 2 is $1/2$ the probability of drawing a number divisible by 3 is $1/3$, and the probability of drawing a number divisible by 6 is $1/6$. What is the probability of drawing a number which is divisible either by 2 or by 3?

C. General Problems

6. Two machines operate in a factory. The probability that machine A will last for another 4 years is 0.2, while the probability that machine B will last for another 4 years is 0.25. Find the probability that:

   i) Both machines will be operating in four years time.

   ii) Neither machine will be operating in four years time.

   iii) At least one machine will be operating in four years time.

7. Two dice are thrown simultaneously. What is the probability that

    i) the total score will be 3?

    ii) the total score will be 7?

8. Four machines, a drill, a lathe, a grinder and a miller operate independently of each other, Their utilizations are: Drill 50%, lathe 40%, miller 70%, grinder 80%.

    i) What is the chance of both drill and lathe not being used at any interval of time?

    ii) What is the chance of all machines being busy?

    iii) What is the chance of all machines being idle?

9. An assembly is made up as follows: 2 of component X, 2 of component Y, 2 of component Z. The percentage of defectives in the large batches supplied to the assembler are: X: 5%, Y: 2%, Z: 10%. On the assumption that the assembly is acceptable only if all component parts are without defect.

    i) What proportion of assemblies will be acceptable?

    ii) What proportion of assemblies will be unacceptable?

10. A piece of equipment will only function if three components A, B and C are all working. The probability of A failing during one year is 5%, that of B failing is 15% and that of C failing is 10%.

    i) What is the probability that the equipment will fail before the end of one year?

    ii) What is the probability that exactly one component will fail during the first year?

11. Three groups of students contain respectively:

    Group A: 3 economists and 1 accountant

    Group B: 2 economists and 2 accountants

    Group C: 1 economist and 3 accountants

    One student is selected from each group. Find the probability that the three students selected will be 1 economist and 2 accountants.

12. A large batch of components is 5% defective. If 5 are tested what is the probability that:

    i) no defective component will occur?

    ii) the test sample will contain

    a) exactly one defective component,

    b) exactly two defective components.

13. i) Explain the meaning (in a statistical context) of the following terms:–

    a) Mutually Exclusive

    b) Independent

    c) Conditional Probability

    ii) If events A and B are mutually exclusive, and events A and C are independent, show that:

    $P(A \text{ or } B) - P(B) = P(A/C)$

iii) When asked about prospects for the future, an economist replied that the probability that business conditions will improve is $1/2$, the probability that they will not remain the same is $2/3$, and the probability that they will not get worse is $3/4$. Discuss the consistency of these probabilities.

iv) A contractor submits 2 tenders for jobs with two different firms. (i.e. one tender with each firm). He estimates his chances of success as $1/4$ and $1/3$ respectively. If the tenders are independent of each other in all respects, calculate the probability that he will be successful in exactly one of them.

14. A firm's requisitions for three basic materials were regularly in error, with probabilities 0.4, 0.3 and 0.2 respectively. Each of the errors was independent of the others because of different amounts and forms by which they were requisitioned.

   For three requisitions, each ordering a different raw material, determine the probabilities of:

   a) errors in all three

   b) errors in at least two

   c) errors in all three, given an error in at least one

   d) errors in two, given an error in at least one.

15. A salesman for a company sells two products, A and B. During a morning he makes three calls on customers. If the chance that he makes a sale of product A is 1 in 3 and the chance that he makes a sale of product B is 1 in 4, and assuming that the sale of product A is independent of the sale of product B, calculate the probability that the salesman will:

   i) Sell both product A and product B at the first call.

   ii) Sell one product at the first call.

   iii) Make no sales of product A in the morning.

   iv) Make at least one sale of product B in the morning.

16. The probability that a new marketing approach will be successful is assessed as being 0.6. The probability that the expenditure for developing this approach can be kept within the original budget is 0.5. The probability that both of these objectives will be achieved is estimated at 0.3. What is the probability that:

   a) at least one of these objectives will be achieved?

   b) the new marketing approach will be successful given that the development cost was kept within the original budget?

   Determine whether these objectives are dependent or independent.

17. a) i) Give one example of two events which are *not* mutually exclusive but which are dependent.

   ii) Give one example of two events which are *not* mutually exclusive but which are independent.

   b) A businessman boards a 6–engine aircraft (three engines on each side) to attend a summit meeting. The probability of an engine failure is estimated to be 0.1 and each engine operates independently of the others.

   If at least one operating engine is needed on each side for the aircraft to fly, what is the probability that the businessman will be absent from the summit meeting due to a crash of the aircraft?

18. The probability that a student will study for all examinations is 0.2. If the student does study, the probability of passing is 0.8. If the student does not study, the probability of passing is only 0.5.

    i)   What is the probability that the student will pass all examinations?

    ii) Given that the student passed, what is the probability that the student did study?

Short Answers

1. a) $^2/_{52}$ b) $^{12}/_{52}$ c) $^{20}/_{52}$ d) $^{13}/_{52}$

2. a) $^{42}/_{60}$ b) $^{48}/_{60}$ c) $^{58}/_{60}$

3. a) and e)

4. 0.65

5. $^2/_3$

6. i) $^1/_2$

   ii) $^3/_5$

   iii) $^2/_5$

7. i) $^1/_{18}$

   ii) $^1/_6$

8. i) 0.3

   ii) 0.112

   iii) 0.018

9. i) 0.70

   ii) 0.30

10. i) 0.27325

    ii) 0.24725

11. $^{13}/_{32}$

12. i) 0.77

    ii) a) 0.20

       b) 0.02

13. i) a) Events A and B are mutually exclusive if $P(AB) = 0$

     b) Events A and B are independent if $P(A/B) = P(A)$

     c) The probability that event B happens, given that event A has already happened, is written $P(B/A)$. This is referred to as conditional probability.

   ii) Events A and B are mutually exclusive

$$\therefore P(AB) = 0$$

Events A and C are independent

$$\therefore P(A/C) = P(A)$$

Now $P(A \text{ or } B) = P(A) + P(B) - P(AB)$

Since $P(AB) = 0$

$$\therefore P(A + B) = P(A) + P(B)$$

$$\therefore P(A + B) - P(B) = P(A)$$

now since $P(A) = P(A/C)$

$$\therefore P(A + B) - P(B) = P(A/C)$$

   iii) A: Conditions improve

B: Conditions remain the same

C: Conditions get worse

$P(A \text{ or } B \text{ or } C) = P(A + B + C)$
$$= P(A) + P(B) + P(C)$$
$$= 1$$

$P(A) = ^1/_2$, $P(\bar{B}) = ^2/_3$, $P(\bar{C}) = ^3/_4$

$P(B) = 1 - P(\bar{B}) = 1 - ^2/_3 = ^1/_3$

$P(C) = 1 - P(\bar{C}) = 1 - ^3/_4 = ^1/_4$

For the given probabilities:

$P(A) + P(B) + P(C) = ^3/_4 + ^1/_3 + ^1/_4$

This is greater than 1 therefore these probabilities are inconsistent.

   iv) $^5/_{12}$

14. a) 0.024

    b) 0.212

    c) 0.036

    d) 0.283

15. i) $^1/_{12}$

    ii) $^5/_{12}$

    iii) $^8/_{27}$

    iv) $^{37}/_{64}$

16. a) 0.8

    b) 0.6

17. a) i) Suppose a box contains 3 white balls and 5 red balls. Two balls are drawn randomly and without replacement. Now define the following events:

A: First ball drawn is white

B: Second ball drawn is white

(17. cont.)

These events are not mutually exclusive but they are dependent.

ii) Suppose a coin is tossed and a die rolled (both are unbiased). Now define the following events:

A: head on coin

B: Six on die

These events are not mutually exclusive and are independent.

b) 0.002

18. i) 0.56

    ii) 0.286

10 Probability Distributions

1. Introduction

The theory of probability, introduced in the last chapter, is developed in this chapter to introduce the concept of random variables and probability distributions. Particular examples of important probability distributions will be considered in later chapters.

2. Random Variable

By definition, a variable can take a range of values. When the variation in the value taken by the variable is due solely to chance (ie is unpredictable), the variable is referred to as a 'random variable'. Examples of random variables are 'the number of heads obtained when a coin is flipped 10 times', 'the score obtained when an unbiased die is thrown', 'number of motorway accidents during a particular time period', 'the number of defective items produced by a manufacturing process', etc.

Two types of random variable are considered in this chapter – continuous and discrete. A 'continuous' random variable is one that can take any value in a given interval (in particular it can take all fractional values). A 'discrete' random variable is one that can only take certain values in a given interval eg the variable can only take whole number values. Both discrete variables and continuous variables will be considered in the following chapters.

In section 2, below, the concept of random variables is developed to introduce probability distributions, initially with reference to frequency distributions.

3. Relative Frequency

From a frequency distribution we can calculate the relative frequency which, in turn, provides an estimate of the probability of occurrence for each value of x (or range of values of x). The relative frequency, which was introduced in chapter 9, is calculated by dividing each value of the frequency by the total frequency. This is illustrated in the following example.

Example

Consider the following frequency distribution which represents the sales of T.V. sets at a discount store over a period of 310 days, and which illustrates the calculation of relative frequencies.

X: Number of T.V. sets sold per day at a discount store (over a period of 310 days).

N.B. X is a discrete variable – it only takes whole number values.

x	f	Relative frequency i.e. $P(X = x)$
0	160	$\frac{160}{310} = 0.516$
1	80	$\frac{80}{310} = 0.258$
2	40	0.129
3	20	0.065
4	10	0.032
	310	1.000

The first two columns here define our frequency distribution which has an arithmetic mean of $\bar{x} = 0.839$.

The third column is the relative frequency which provides us with an estimate of the probability associated with each value of x.

For example $P(X = 1) = 0.258$

Based on the period of 310 days, assuming that this period was generally representative of sales of T.V. sets and that conditions do not change, we can expect that the percentage of days on which exactly 1 TV set is sold will equal 25.8% (in the long run).

N.B.

It is important to distinguish between X and x in the expression $P(X = x)$.

X   denotes the variable under consideration (expressed in words)

x   denotes the values that X can take so that $P(X = x)$ is notation for the probability that X (i.e. the number of T.V. sets sold per day at a discount store) equals the number x.

For example, $P(X = 2)$ means the probability that the number of T.V. sets sold per day equals 2.

4. Probability Distributions

If we tabulate the probabilities of occurrence for each possible value (or range of possible values) of the variable X then we have a probability distribution. (N.B. The sum of all the probabilities given in a probability distribution must equal 1.)

Consider, again, the following example:

X: Number of T.V. sets sold per day at a discount store

x	P(X=x)
0	0.516
1	0.258
2	0.129
3	0.065
4	0.032
	1.000

Here we have a probability distribution and from this probability distribution we can calculate the 'expected number of T.V. sets sold per day'.

4.1 Expected Value

Given the probability distribution of a variable X, we can calculate the expected value of the variable X which is defined as:

$$E(X) = \Sigma x P(X=x)$$

The calculation and interpretation of E(X) is illustrated in the following examples.

Example

X: Number of T.V. sets sold per day at a discount store

x	$P(X=x)$	$xP(X=x)$
0	0.516	0
1	0.258	0.258
2	0.129	0.258
3	0.065	0.195
4	0.032	0.128
	1.000	0.839

$$E(X) = \sum xP(X=x) = \mathbf{0.839}$$

The third column, headed ' $xP(X=x)$ ', is obtained by multiplying together each value of x (in column 1) by its associated probability (given in column 2).

Note that E(X) is obtained by summing the values of the third column.

We can thus say that the expected number of T.V. sets sold per day at the discount store is 0.839. Now clearly it is not possible to sell 0.839 sets on any one day, and that on any particular day the number of T.V. sets sold will be 0 or 1 or 2 ......etc.

The interpretation of E(X) = 0.839 is that over a long period of time the average sales per day will be 0.839.

N.B. the value of E(X) is the same as the value of a in our original frequency distribution described in section 2. (This will always be the case).

Example

Let X = outcome resulting from the throw of a six–sided die.

x	$P(X=x)$	$xP(X=x)$
1	$1/6$	$1/6$
2	$1/6$	$2/6$
3	$1/6$	$3/6$
4	$1/6$	$4/6$
5	$1/6$	$5/6$
6	$1/6$	$6/6$
	1	$21/6$

Hence we have that $E(X) = {}^{21}/_6 = \mathbf{3.5}$

Again we can note that it is not possible to obtain an outcome of 3.5 in any single throw of the die. However, in the long run (i.e. after a large number of throws), the outcomes will average out to be 3.5.

Example

Suppose in a game of rolling a die you are to receive £6 every time you roll a six and pay out £1 every time you do not. What is your expected gain per game?

Let Y: Your pay–off per game.

Then we have:

y	$P(Y=y)$	$yP(Y=y)$
-1	$5/6$	$-5/6$
6	$1/6$	$6/6$
	1	$1/6$

(N.B. if you lose a game, you lose £1 and your pay–off is –1.)

$E(Y) = £ 1/6$

We can conclude that if we play the game a large number of times we can expect to have, on average, a gain of £ $1/6$ per game (even though the probability of losing £1 is $5/6$ each time we play the game).

Example

Consider the following game:

One card is drawn from a pack of ordinary playing cards.

If the card is an Ace, player A wins £4 from player B.

If the card is a picture card, player A wins £2 from player B otherwise player A loses £1 to player B.

Calculate the expected gain or loss for Player A if the game is played 100 times (with the card being replaced after each draw).

Let X: Amount won (or lost) by Player A in one game.

x	$P(X=x)$	$xP(X = x)$
4	$4/52$	$16/52$
2	$12/52$	$24/52$
-1	$36/52$	$-36/52$
	1	$4/52$

$E(X) = \sum x \, P(X=x) = 4/52$

Therefore Player A has an expected gain of £$4/52$ per game.

If 100 games are played, Player A can expect to win £$4/52$ x 100 = £$400/52$ = **£7.69.**

4.2 A Business Application

A practical application of expectation is illustrated in the following exam

A research agency observes the following pattern of demand for its servic

No. of researchers required x	No. of days x researchers required	
10	1	
11	5	
12	10	} 41
13	17	
14	8	
15	5	
16	4	
	———	
	50	

Now the agency can either have permanent staff at a cost of £40 per day per research
contract the work at a cost of £80 per day. If the agency employs 14 permanent staff, wh
be the cost per day if the demand pattern continues?

From the frequency data above, we would expect that the work could be a handled
permanent staff on 41 days out of the next 50 (i.e. on 82% of future days), at a cost of £4
researcher per day. Similarly, one extra researcher at £80 per day would be required on 1(
future days, and two on 8% of future days.

This can be summarized in the following table:

X: Number of researchers required per day

Y: Number of extra (sub–contracted) researchers required

No. researchers required per day x	P(X=x)	No. of extra researchers y	P(Y=y)		Expectation yP(Y=y)
10	0.02	0	0.02		0
11	0.1	0	0.1		0
12	0.2	0	0.2	} 0.82	0
13	0.34	0	0.34		0
14	0.16	0	0.16		0
15	0.1	1	0.1		0.1
16	0.08	2	0.08		0.16
					———
					0.26

So *on average* we would expect 0.26 extra (ie subcontracted) researchers to be required per day. The
total cost per day would then be £40 x 14 for staff, plus 0.26 x £80 for temporary researchers. That
is, £580.80 per day.

rk out the cost per day for different numbers of permanent staff, and
oy that in the long run would minimise the expected cost (always
attern does not alter).

nswers on page 110)

ossed three times. Each time a head is thrown we are paid 5p, each time a tail is
ose 3p. What is our expected gain in this game?

lar game there are 4 possible outcomes with the following pay–offs and probability.

ome	I	II	III	IV
–off (in £)	25	–40	16	–8
bability	0.4	0.2	0.2	0.2

the expected value of the pay–off in each game?

ollowing grouped frequency distribution represents the hours per week worked by a
-time worker over the past 50 weeks.

Hours/week	No. of weeks
0 – 9	8
10 – 19	12
20 – 29	15
30 – 39	13
40 – 49	2

If the worker gets paid £3 per hour, calculate the workers expected pay per week.

4. In a business venture a company estimates that it can make a profit of £300 with probability of
    0.6, or take a loss of £100 with probability 0.4. Find the company's expectation.

5. If a man purchases a raffle ticket he can win a £5000 1st prize with probability 0.001, or a 2nd
    prize of £2000 with probability 0.003. What would be a fair price to pay for the ticket?

6. Calculate a heating firm's expected annual revenue resulting from the sales of central heating
    systems if the average system is priced at £1200 and the probability distribution of yearly sales
    is given by:

Sales (ie No of Systems)	Probability
40 – 59	0.05
60 – 79	0.10
80 – 99	0.10
100 – 119	0.30
120 – 149	0.25
150 – 199	0.20

7. A bag contains 2 white balls and 3 black balls. Four people, A,B,C, and D, in the order named, each draw one ball and do not replace it. The first to draw a white ball receives £10. If each player initially pays £2.50 to play the game (which is not returned whatever the outcome of the game), determine each player's expectation.

8. A firm has obtained contracts for the supply of a large quantity of a particular engineering component to three firms A, B, and C. The contracts include penalty clauses for failing to make delivery on the agreed date. To be able to meet these dates, different production methods have to be employed for each contract. The firms resources are such that only one contract can be satisfied at any one time.

   Contract A would require stock–piling, contract B would permit normal production methods, and contract C would require the hiring of additional equipment and labour, hence profits are affected.

   The following table gives the profits, penalties and probabilities that the penalties might occur.

	Profit	Penalty	Probability that delivery date cannot be met
A	£10,000	£3,000	0.4
B	£12,000	£6,000	0.2
C	£11,000	£4,000	0.3

   By considering the expected return on the individual contracts, give advice to the manager on whether he should stock–pile, continue normal production or hire additional resources.

9. A particular engineering component costs £10 to assemble if done on the premises with existing staff. If, however, it is subcontracted to an outside firm it costs £15.

   The following demand pattern has been observed over a period of 100 days:

   No. required per day: 0 1 2 3 4 5

   No. of days: 25 30 24 14 5 2

   a) If the policy of the firm is to replenish the stock up to two assemblies per day and to subcontract any requirements beyond this number, what is the expected cost of this scheme.

   b) What is the probability of a stock–out per day (i.e. the probability that work has to be sub–contracted).

Short Answers

1. 1.3 pence

2. £3.60

3. £66.90

4. £140

5. £11

6. £143,700

7. Expectations for Players A, B, C, D respectively are:

   £1.50; £0.50; –£0.50; –£1.50;

8. Go for Contract B

9. a) £16.50

   b) 0.21

11 The Binomial Distribution

1. Introduction

In this chapter a particular probability distribution, the Binomial Distribution, is considered. The Binomial Distribution is a discrete probability distribution (ie the variable takes discrete values) and forms a basis for a range of business applications eg Quality Control.

2. Binomial Experiment

Consider the following experiment:

a) There are a series of n independent trials, each trial having only two possible mutually exclusive outcomes (often referred to as 'success' and 'failure').

b) The probability of a 'success' occurring remains the same from trial to trial.

Such an experiment is called a 'binomial experiment.'

Example

Consider the experiment of flipping a coin, say, 5 times.

i) This experiment consists of 5 trials (ie each 'flip' of the coin represents a trial), so we have n = 5.

ii) Each trial (ie flip of the coin) is independent of any other trial.

iii) Each trial has only two possible mutually exclusive outcomes (i.e. 'head' or 'tail').

iv) The probability of obtaining a particular outcome in a trial (eg a 'head') remains the same from trial to trial.

3. Binomial Distribution

If a random variable, X say, is defined as the number of 'successes' (or 'failures') that occur in a binomial experiment, then the probability distribution of X is said to be a 'binomial distribution'.

The binomial distribution is a discrete probability distribution (i.e. the random variable only takes integer values).

The probability function for the binomial distribution (i.e. that function which enables us to calculate the probability of occurrence of any value of the random variable X) is given by.

$$P(X = x) = {}^nC_x \, p^x(1-p)^{n-x} \qquad x = 0,1,.... \, n$$

where   n = number of trials

p = probability of obtaining a 'success' in a single trial.

x = a particular value of X.

and where

$${}^nC_x = \frac{n!}{x!(n-x)!} \quad \text{with} \quad n! = n(n-1)(n-2).....$$

Note that the binomial distribution is defined by the values of n and p (i.e. once we know the values of n and p we are in a position to evaluate all the probabilities for the random variable X) and that the random variable X takes only integer values in the range 0 to n inclusive (i.e. x = 0,1,....n).

The mean of the binomial distribution [ie E(x)] is equal to np.

The standard deviation is equal to $\sqrt{npq}$ where q = 1–p

Example

If we again consider the binomial experiment where a coin is flipped 5 times, and define X as follows:

X: Number of heads obtained

n = 5

p = $^1/_2$

and x = 0, 1,....n (ie x can take values 0,1,...5)

i) The probability that 3 heads are obtained (in 5 flips of a coin) is given by:

$P(X = 3)$ = $^5C_3$ $(0.5)^3(0.5)^{5-3}$

$$= \frac{5!}{3!(5-3)!} (0.5)^3(0.5)^2$$

$$= \frac{5 \times 4 \times 3 \times 2 \times 1}{3 \times 2 \times 1 \times 2 \times 1} (0.5)^5$$

$$= 10(0.5)^5 = \mathbf{0.3125}$$

ii) The probability that 1 head is obtained (in 5 flips of a coin) is given by:

$P(X = 1)$ = $^5C_1$ $(0.5)^1(0.5)^{5-1}$

$$= \frac{5!}{1!(5-1)!} (0.5)^1(0.5)^4$$

$$= \frac{5 \times 4 \times 3 \times 2 \times 1}{1 \times 4 \times 3 \times 2 \times 1} (0.5)^5$$

$$= 5(0.5)^5 = \mathbf{0.1563}$$

iii) The probability that 0 heads are obtained (in 5 flips of a coin) is given by:

$P(X = 0)$ = $^5C_0$ $(0.5)^0(0.5)^{5-0}$

$$= \frac{5!}{0!(5-0)!} (0.5)^0(0.5)^5$$

Now 0! = 1 and any number to the power 0 also equals 1.

Therefore

$$P(X = 0) = \frac{5!}{0! \, 5!} (0.5)^0 (0.5)^5$$

$$= \frac{5 \times 4 \times 3 \times 2 \times 1}{1 \times 5 \times 4 \times 3 \times 2 \times 1} (0.5)^5$$

$$= (0.5)^5 = \mathbf{0.03125}$$

Similarly we could calculate $P(X = 2)$, and $P(X = 5)$ and hence we would have generated the probability distribution for x which is given by:

x	$p(X = x)$
0	0.0312
1	0.1563
2	0.3125
3	0.3125
4	0.1563
5	0.0312
	1.0000

The mean of the binomial probability distribution (i.e the expected value of X) is given by np. Therefore we have mean = np = 5(0.5) = 2.5

Also Standard deviation $= \sqrt{np(1-p)} = \sqrt{5(0.5)(0.5)} = 1.118$

Example

Metal components are subjected to rigorous breaking tests. The probability that a component will break during such a test is 0.40. If 4 such components are tested on one particular occasion, what is the probability that:

i) 3 of them will break?

ii) 2, 3 or 4 will break?

iii) 0 or 1 will break?

Solution

First we define X as follows:

X: Number of components that will break during the test

n = 4

p = 0.4

$P(X = x) = {}^nC_x \, p^x (q)^{n-x}$ where $q = 1 - p$

i) $P(X = 3) = {}^4C_3 \, (0.4)^3 (0.6)^1$

$$= \frac{4!}{3! \, 1!} (0.4)^3 (0.6)^1$$

$$= 4(0.4)^3 (0.6)$$

$$= \mathbf{0.1536}$$

ii) P(X = 2, 3 or 4) = P(X=2) + P(X=3) + P(X=4)

now P(X=2) and P(X=4) can be calculated in the same way as P(X=3) was calculated in (i).

We would then have:

P(X=2, 3 or 4)   = P(X=2) + P(X=3) + P(X=4)

         = 0.3456 + 0.1536 + 0.0256

         = 0.5248

iii) P(X=0 or 1) = P(X = 0) + P(X = 1)

However, in this example, we can make use of the following:

P(X=0) + P(X=1) + P(X=2) + P(X=3) + P(X=4) = 1

Therefore we have:

P(X=0 or 1)   = P(X=0) + P(X=1)

   = 1 – P(X=2) – P(X=3) – P(X=4)

   = 1 – [P(X=2) + P(X=3) + P(X=4)]

   = 1 – 0.5248 (from (ii))

   = 0.4752

Appendix

Combinations

The probability of obtaining a six in one throw of a standard die equals $1/6$.

If we wished to calculate the probability of obtaining one six in three throws of a standard die we could proceed as follows using the addition and multiplication laws of probability:

We first define:

S: obtaining a six in a single throw of a die

$\bar{S}$: not obtaining a six in a single throw of a die

In throwing a die 3 times, the possible ways of obtaining six are as follows:

$S\bar{S}\bar{S}$ or $\bar{S}S\bar{S}$ or $\bar{S}\,\bar{S}S$

Hence the probability of obtaining a six in 3 throws of a die equals:

$P(S\,\bar{S}\,\bar{S}) + P(\bar{S}\,S\,\bar{S}) + P(\bar{S}\,\bar{S}\,S)$

Now as $P(S) = 1/6$, $P(\bar{S}) = 5/6$,

and each throw is independent of any other throw, we have:

Probability of obtaining a six in 3 throws of a die $= [1/6 \times 5/6 \times 5/6] + [5/6 \times 1/6 \times 5/6] + [5/6 \times 5/6 \times 1/6]$
$= 3[1/6][5/6]^2 = 0.3472$

(This is an example where the binomial distribution is applicable).

In this example, instead of listing the 3 possible ways of obtaining one six (when a die is thrown 3 times) – which would have been far more tedious and difficult had we been dealing with larger numbers (e.g. the probability of obtaining 4 sixes in 20 throws of a die) – we could have calculated the number of possible 'combinations' of one six in three throws using the general expression for calculating such combinations. This is given by:

$$nC_x = \frac{n!}{x!(n-x)!} \quad \text{where } n! = n(n-1)(n-2)\ldots$$

and represents the number of combinations of n events taken x at a time.

In the above example,

n = 3 (ie number of throws of die)

x = 1 (ie number of sixes)

and hence

$$nC_x = 3C_1 = \frac{3!}{1!\,(3-1)!} = \frac{3!}{1!\,2!} = \frac{3\times2\times1}{1\times2\times1} = 3$$

Likewise the number of ways of obtaining 4 sixes in 20 throws of a die would not be easy to list out, but can be calculated by evaluating:

$$20C_4 = \frac{20!}{4!\,(20-4)!} = \frac{20!}{4!\,16!} = \frac{20\times19\times18\times17\times16!}{4\times3\times2\times1\times16!} = 4845$$

Examples of Binomial Distributions

i)   n = 5   ii)   n = 10   iii)   n = 20   iv)   n = 50

p = 0.5   p = 0.25   p = 0.15   p = 0.05

x	$P(x)$		x	$P(x)$		x	$P(x)$		x	$P(x)$
0	.0312		0	.0563		0	.0388		0	.0769
1	.1563		1	.1877		1	.1368		1	.2025
2	.3125		2	.2816		2	.2293		2	.2611
3	.3125		3	.2503		3	.2428		3	.2199
4	.1562		4	.1460		4	.1821		4	.1360
5	.0313		5	.0584		5	.1029		5	.0658
			6	.0162		6	.0454		6	.0260
			7	.0031		7	.0160		7	.0086
			8	.0004		8	.0046		8	.0024
						9	.0011		9	.0006
						10	.0002		10	.0002

v)   n = 5   vi)   n = 10   vii)   n = 20   viii)   n = 50

p = 0.10   p = 0.10   p = 0.10   p = 0.10

x	$P(x)$		x	$P(x)$		x	$P(x)$		x	$P(x)$
0	.5905		0	.3487		0	.1216		0	.0052
1	.3280		1	.3874		1	.2701		1	.0286
2	.0729		2	.1937		2	.2852		2	.0779
3	.0081		3	.0574		3	.1901		3	.1386
4	.0005		4	.0112		4	.0898		4	.1809
			5	.0015		5	.0319		5	.1849
			6	.0001		6	.0089		6	.1541
						7	.0020		7	.1077
						8	.0003		8	.0642
						9	.0001		9	.0334
									10	.0151
									11	.0062
									12	.0022
									13	.0007
									14	.0002
									15	.0001

(These probability distributions are graphically represented on the next page.)

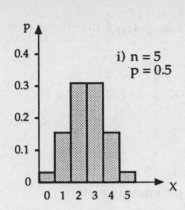

i) n = 5
p = 0.5

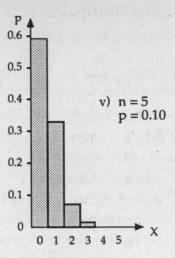

v) n = 5
p = 0.10

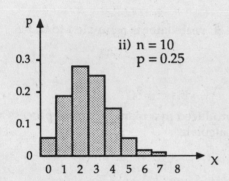

ii) n = 10
p = 0.25

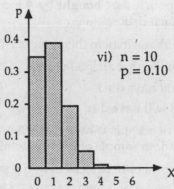

vi) n = 10
p = 0.10

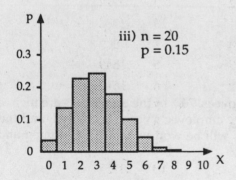

iii) n = 20
p = 0.15

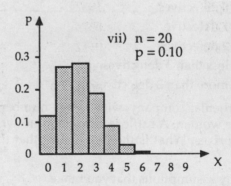

vii) n = 20
p = 0.10

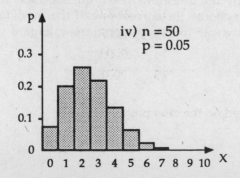

iv) n = 50
p = 0.05

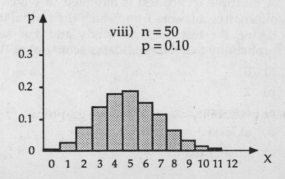

viii) n = 50
p = 0.10

Exercises (*Answers on page 120*)

1. In a large batch of bolts there are 10% defectives. The batch is so large that the chance of obtaining a defective bolt is unaltered by sampling.

    Evaluate the following probabilities for the given sample sizes:

    i) exactly 2 are defective when:

    a) n=5   b) n=6   c) n=10   d) n=20

    ii) at least 3 are defective when n=10

    iii) for n = 5:   more than 2 but less than 4 are defective

     n = 10:   not less than 4 and not more than 6 are defective

     n = 20:   the number of defectives is between (but not including) 14 and 17.

2. Life insurance policies are bought by 4 men in similar employment and having the same age and health characteristics.

    The probability that a man in this category will be alive 30 years later is estimated to be 0.6.

    Find the probability that after 30 years

    a) only two will have died

    b) at least two will have died.

3. From past experience it is known that 8% of the items produced in a manufacturing process are defective. A random sample of twenty items is taken. Calculate:

    i) The mean number of defectives in the sample.

    ii) The probability that the sample contains:

    a) 0 defectives

    b) 1 defective

    c) 2 defectives

    d) less than 3 defectives

    e) more than 2 defectives.

4. In a particular company, with a large number of employees, 70% of the employees are men and 30% are women. A raffle is arranged into which every employee's name is entered, and there are 15 prizes. What is the probability that the prizes will be won by exactly 6 women and 9 men?

    State any assumptions that you make.

5. A multiple choice test is designed in which there are ten questions. Each question has five alternative answers from which the candidate has to choose the correct one. If the candidate taking the test does not study and guesses the answer to every question, calculate the probability that the candidate's score out of 10 is:

    a) 0

    b) 2

    c) less than 2

    d) at least 3

    e) greater than 3.

6. A firm buys component parts in large batches. It has been agreed that a 5% defective rate can be tolerated and that the following inspection scheme will be operated by the firm as the consignments of components arrive.

    Scheme:

    A random sample of size 5 is to be taken. If the sample contains 3 or more defectives, the batch is returned to the manufacturer for replacement. If the sample contains not more than 1 defective, the whole batch is accepted as satisfactory. If however the sample taken contains exactly 2 defectives a second sample is taken. If this again contains two or more defectives, the whole batch is returned for replacement, if it contains less than two defectives the batch is accepted as satisfactory.

    Define X as the number of defectives in a sample of size 5. Given that a batch does *in fact* contain 5% defectives, the sampling distribution for X follows the binomial distribution with:

    p = P(obtaining a defective) = 0.05.

    The distribution is given below:

x	P(X = x)
0	.7738
1	.2036
2	.0214
3	.0011
4	.0001
5	.0000
	1.0000

    Find:

    a) the probability that a batch will be returned after one inspection only

    b) the probability that the batch will be accepted after one inspection

    c) the probability that a second inspection will take place.

    d) the probability that a batch will be accepted.

7. A firm manufactures electric kettles. The probability that a kettle is faulty is 0.10. Kettles are packed in boxes of 5. A consignment of 500 such boxes is sent to a wholesaler. How many boxes are likely to contain exactly 2 faulty kettles?

8. A firm's internal auditor knows from past experience that the probability of a particular voucher being completed incorrectly is 0.15. Assuming that errors occur independently, calculate the probability that if three vouchers are chosen randomly from a large batch

    a) all three are completed *correctly*

    b) exactly two are completed *correctly*

    c) exactly one is completed *incorrectly*

    d) at least one is completed *incorrectly*.

Short Answers

1. i) 0.0729 (for n=5)

     0.0934 (for n=6)

     0.1937 (for n=10)

     0.2852 (for n=20)

   ii) 0.0702

   iii) 0.0081; 0.0128; 0 approx;

2. a) 0.3456

   b) 0.5248

3. i) 1.6

   ii) a) 0.1887

      b) 0.3282

      c) 0.2710

      d) 0.7879

      e) 0.2121

4. 0.1472

5. a) 0.1074

   b) 0.3020

   c) 0.3758

   d) 0.3222

   e) 0.1209

6. a) 0.0012

   b) 0.9774

   c) 0.0214

   d) 0.9983

7. 0.0729

8. a) 0.6141

   b) 0.3251

   c) 0.003375

   d) 0.3859

12 The Normal Distribution

1. Introduction

In this chapter one of the most important probability distributions in statistics, the normal distribution, is considered. The normal distribution is a continuous probability distribution (ie the variable takes continuous values) and is the most useful and commonly used of all probability distributions.

2. Properties

The normal distribution is a continuous probability distribution with the mean denoted by the Greek letter μ, and the standard deviation denoted by the Greek letter σ.

It is a symmetrical bell–shaped distribution with mean = median = mode.

A random variable X, which follows a normal distribution with mean μ and standard deviation σ, is denoted as $X \sim N(\mu, \sigma^2)$.

(NB σ^2 denotes the variance of X).

The distribution of X can be graphically represented as follows:

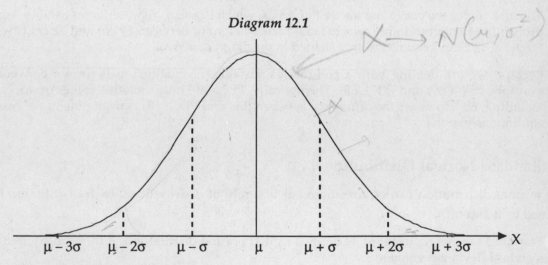

Diagram 12.1

X takes values between $-\infty$ and $+\infty$.

The area under the curve and above the X axis equals 1. It follows that the area on either side of the perpendicular line passing through the mean equals 0.5.

The Normal distribution has the following properties:

68.26% of the distribution lies within $\pm 1\sigma$ of μ

95.45% of the distribution lies within $\pm 2\sigma$ of μ

99.74% of the distribution lies within $\pm 3\sigma$ of μ

These properties can be illustrated by the following example:

X: height of children (in cm) in a particular school.

$\mu = 66 \; \sigma = 3$ [ie $X \sim N(66, 3^2)$]

Diagram 12.2

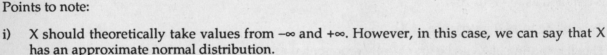

Approximately 68% of children have a height between 63 and 69 cm

Approximately 95% of children have a height between 60 and 72 cm

Approximately 99% of children have a height between 57 and 75 cm

Points to note:

i)   X should theoretically take values from $-\infty$ and $+\infty$. However, in this case, we can say that X has an approximate normal distribution.

ii) The area under the curve and above the X axis, which equals 1, represents probability. e.g. The probability that a randomly selected child has a height of between 69 cm and 72 cm is written $P(69 < X < 72)$ and equals the area shaded in the diagram above.

iii) Because we are dealing with a continuous variable, no distinction is drawn between, for example, $P(X > 69)$ and $P(X \geq 69)$. Theoretically, $P(X > 69)$ only includes values up to, but not including, 69. However the difference between this and $P(X \geq 69)$ is negligible in the case of a continuous variable.

3. Standard Normal Distribution

The normal distribution can be considered as a family of distributions, each distribution being defined by μ and σ.

The Standard normal distribution is defined as that normal distribution with mean equal to zero and standard deviation equal to 1.

The random variable having a standard normal distribution is usually denoted by the letter Z.

The probabilities associated with the Standard Normal distribution (ie areas under the Standard Normal curve) are tabulated (see page 127).

From tables we can read off the probability that $0 \leq Z \leq z$, as illustrated in Diagram 12.3, where z is a particular value of the variable Z.

Diagram 12.3

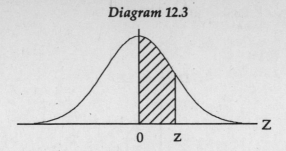

$P(0 \leq Z \leq z)$ = shaded area.

Examples of the use of 'Standard normal' tables (page 127) are given below:

i) $P(0 \leq Z \leq 1.2) = \mathbf{0.3849}$

Diagram 12.4

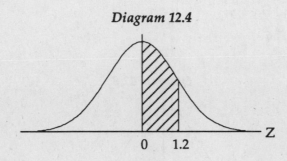

ii) $P(0 \leq Z \leq 2.23) = \mathbf{0.4871}$

Diagram 12.5

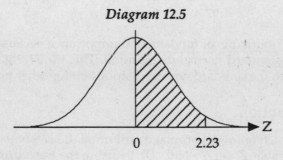

iii) $P(Z \geq 0.95)$ $= 0.5 - P(0 \leq Z \leq 0.95)$
          $= 0.5 - 0.3289$
          $= \mathbf{0.1711}$

Diagram 12.6

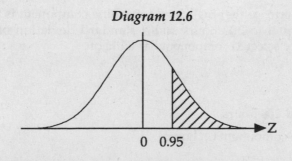

iv) P(1.1 ≤ Z ≤ 1.85) = P(0 ≤ Z ≤ 1.85) – P(0 ≤ Z ≤ 1.1)

   = 0.4678 – 0.3643

   = **0.1035**

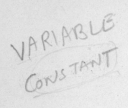
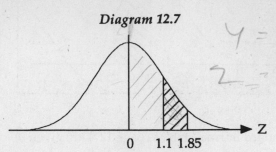

Diagram 12.7

VARIABLE
CONSTANT

0   1.1 1.85

v) P(Z ≤ –1.97) = P(Z ≥ 1.97)

   = 0.5 – P(0 ≤ Z ≤ 1.97)

   = 0.5 – 0.4756

   = **0.0244**

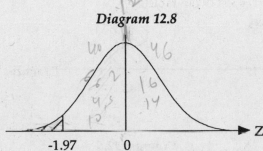

Diagram 12.8

–1.97   0

The Standard Normal Distribution is of fundamental importance because any normal distribution can be transformed to the standard normal distribution. This transformation allows us to use the probabilities associated with the standard normal distribution for other normal distributions.

4. The Normal Distribution

Any random variable X which follows a normal distribution (ie X ~ N(μ , σ²)) can be transformed to the standard normal variable Z (ie Z ~ N(0 , 1)) by using the transformation:

$$Z = \frac{X - \mu}{\sigma}$$

Example

It is known from past experience that the life of a machine component is approximately normally distributed with mean equal to 200 hours and a standard deviation of 4 hours. Calculate the probability that a randomly selected component has a life of:

i)   at least 206 hours

ii) less than 198 hours

iii) between 204 hours and 208 hours.

   X: life of the machine component (in hours)

   X ~ N(200 , 4²)

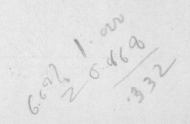

i) We require P(X ≥ 206)

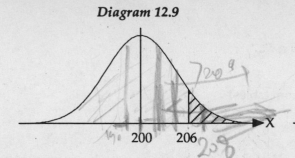

Diagram 12.9

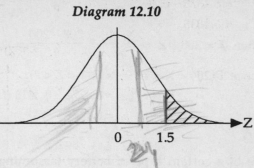

Diagram 12.10

$$Z = \frac{X - \mu}{\sigma}$$

When X = 206, $Z = \frac{206 - 200}{4} = \frac{6}{4} = 1.5$

Hence P(X ≥ 206) = P (Z ≥ 1.5)

= 0.5 − 0.4332 (from tables)

= **0.0668**

ii) We require P(X < 198)

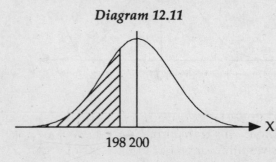

Diagram 12.11

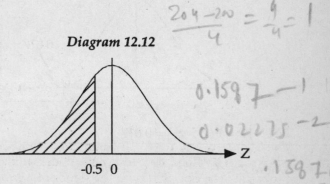

Diagram 12.12

When X = 198, $Z = \frac{X - \mu}{\sigma} = \frac{198 - 200}{4} = \frac{-2}{4} = -0.5$

Hence P(X < 198) = P (Z < −0.5)

= 0.5 − 0.1915 (from tables)

= **0.3085**

iii) We require P(204 < X < 208)

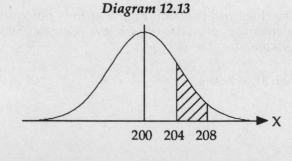

Diagram 12.13

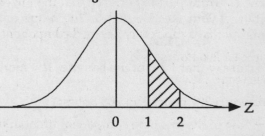

Diagram 12.14

When $X = 204$, $Z = \dfrac{X - \mu}{\sigma} = \dfrac{204 - 200}{4} = 1$

When $X = 208$, $Z = \dfrac{X - \mu}{\sigma} = \dfrac{208 - 200}{4} = 2$

Hence $P(204 < X < 208) = P(1 < Z < 2)$
$$= 0.4772 - 0.3413 \text{ (from tables)}$$
$$= \mathbf{0.1359}$$

Example

The life of a certain type of battery (assuming continuous use) is known to be approximately normally distributed with mean 30 hours and standard deviation 30 minutes. If 1.7% of the batteries last more than 'K' hours, find the value of K.

X: life of batteries (in hours)

$X \sim N(30, 0.5^2)$

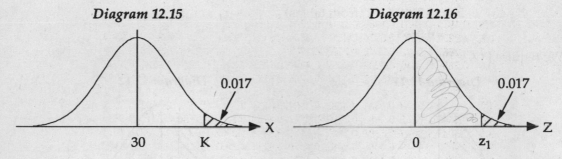

Diagram 12.15   Diagram 12.16

$P(X > K) = P(Z > z_1) = 0.017$

where $Z = \dfrac{X - \mu}{\sigma}$

From tables we see that $z_1 = 2.12$

Now $Z = \dfrac{X - \mu}{\sigma}$

therefore we have

$$2.12 = \frac{K - 30}{0.5}$$

$$0.5\,(2.12) = K - 30$$

$$1.06 = K - 30$$

$$K = \mathbf{31.06}$$

$\therefore$ We can say that 1.7% of the batteries last more than 31.06 hours.

Areas under the Standard Normal curve

i.e. P(0 ≤ Z ≤ z)

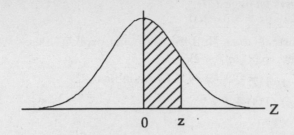

z	0.00	0.01	0.02	0.03	0.04	0.05	0.06	0.07	0.08	0.09
0.0	0.0000	0.0040	0.0080	0.0120	0.0160	0.0199	0.0239	0.0279	0.0319	0.0359
0.1	0.0398	0.0438	0.0478	0.0517	0.0557	0.0596	0.0636	0.0675	0.0714	0.0754
0.2	0.0793	0.0832	0.0871	0.0910	0.0948	0.0987	0.1026	0.1064	0.1103	0.1141
0.3	0.1179	0.1217	0.1255	0.1293	0.1331	0.1368	0.1406	0.1443	0.1480	0.1517
0.4	0.1554	0.1591	0.1628	0.1664	0.1700	0.1736	0.1772	0.1808	0.1844	0.1879
0.5	0.1915	0.1950	0.1985	0.2019	0.2054	0.2088	0.2123	0.2157	0.2190	0.2224
0.6	0.2258	0.2291	0.2324	0.2357	0.2389	0.2422	0.2454	0.2486	0.2518	0.2549
0.7	0.2580	0.2612	0.2642	0.2673	0.2704	0.2734	0.2764	0.2794	0.2823	0.2852
0.8	0.2881	0.2910	0.2939	0.2967	0.2996	0.3023	0.3051	0.3078	0.3106	0.3133
0.9	0.3159	0.3186	0.3212	0.3238	0.3264	0.3289	0.3315	0.3340	0.3365	0.3389
1.0	0.3413	0.3438	0.3461	0.3485	0.3508	0.3531	0.3554	0.3577	0.3599	0.3621
1.1	0.3643	0.3665	0.3686	0.3708	0.3729	0.3749	0.3770	0.3790	0.3810	0.3830
1.2	0.3849	0.3869	0.3888	0.3907	0.3925	0.3944	0.3962	0.3980	0.3997	0.4015
1.3	0.4032	0.4049	0.4066	0.4082	0.4099	0.4115	0.4131	0.4147	0.4162	0.4177
1.4	0.4192	0.4207	0.4222	0.4236	0.4251	0.4265	0.4279	0.4292	0.4306	0.4319
1.5	0.4332	0.4345	0.4357	0.4370	0.4382	0.4394	0.4406	0.4418	0.4429	0.4441
1.6	0.4452	0.4463	0.4474	0.4484	0.4495	0.4505	0.4515	0.4525	0.4535	0.4545
1.7	0.4554	0.4564	0.4573	0.4582	0.4591	0.4599	0.4608	0.4616	0.4625	0.4633
1.8	0.4641	0.4649	0.4656	0.4664	0.4671	0.4678	0.4686	0.4693	0.4699	0.4706
1.9	0.4713	0.4719	0.4726	0.4732	0.4738	0.4744	0.4750	0.4756	0.4761	0.4767
2.0	0.4772	0.4778	0.4783	0.4788	0.4793	0.4798	0.4803	0.4808	0.4812	0.4817
2.1	0.4821	0.4826	0.4830	0.4834	0.4838	0.4842	0.4846	0.4850	0.4854	0.4857
2.2	0.4861	0.4864	0.4868	0.4871	0.4875	0.4878	0.4881	0.4884	0.4887	0.4890
2.3	0.4893	0.4896	0.4898	0.4901	0.4904	0.4906	0.4909	0.4911	0.4913	0.4916
2.4	0.4918	0.4920	0.4922	0.4925	0.4927	0.4929	0.4931	0.4932	0.4934	0.4936
2.5	0.4938	0.4940	0.4941	0.4943	0.4945	0.4946	0.4948	0.4949	0.4951	0.4952
2.6	0.4953	0.4955	0.4956	0.4957	0.4959	0.4960	0.4961	0.4962	0.4963	0.4964
2.7	0.4965	0.4966	0.4967	0.4968	0.4969	0.4970	0.4971	0.4972	0.4973	0.4974
2.8	0.4974	0.4975	0.4976	0.4977	0.4977	0.4978	0.4979	0.4979	0.4980	0.4981
2.9	0.4981	0.4982	0.4982	0.4983	0.4984	0.4984	0.4985	0.4985	0.4986	0.4986
3.0	0.4987	0.4987	0.4987	0.4988	0.4988	0.4989	0.4989	0.4989	0.4990	0.4990
3.1	0.4990	0.4991	0.4991	0.4991	0.4992	0.4992	0.4992	0.4992	0.4993	0.4993
3.2	0.4993	0.4993	0.4994	0.4994	0.4994	0.4994	0.4994	0.4995	0.4995	0.4995
3.3	0.4995	0.4995	0.4995	0.4996	0.4996	0.4996	0.4996	0.4996	0.4996	0.4997
3.4	0.4997	0.4997	0.4997	0.4997	0.4997	0.4997	0.4997	0.4997	0.4997	0.4998

Exercises (Answers on page 131)

1. Using the Standard Normal tables, find the following probabilities:

   a) $P(Z > 1)$ b) $P(Z > 2.07)$

   c) $P(Z < -1.56)$ d) $P(Z > -1.5)$

   e) $P(Z > 0)$ f) $P(-1 < Z < 2)$

   g) $P(1.57 < Z < 2.1)$

   h) $P(-2.11 < Z < -0.89)$

2. Find, using Standard Normal tables, the value of K for each of the following:

   a) $P(Z > K) = 0.015$

   b) $P(0 < Z < K) = 0.4732$

   c) $P(Z < K) = 0.8212$

   d) $P(Z < K) = 0.006$

3. If the random variable X follows a normal distribution with mean=100 and standard deviation = 5, find the probability that:

   a) $P(X > 107)$ b) $P(X > 98)$

   c) $P(X < 95)$ d) $P(101 < X < 109)$

   e) $P(91 < X < 94)$ f) $P(93 < X < 106)$

4. Suppose that the distribution of women by size of feet is normal, with an arithmetic mean length of 20 cm. and a standard deviation of 2.5cm. A manufacturer of women's shoes has an output of 10,000 pairs per week and wants to know how many pairs of shoes of each length given below to produce. Use the table of the area under a Normal curve to answer the manufacturer's question.

   a) above 21.25 cm.   b) below 16.25 cm.

   c) above 18.75 cm.   d) below 22.5 cm.

5. The daily delivery of mail at a large City firm follows a time pattern conforming to the Normal distribution, with a mean time of arrival at 8.40a.m. and with a Standard Deviation of 20 minutes.

   Estimate the number of occasions during the 250 working days in the year when the mail arrives

   a) before the main gates open at 8.00a.m.

   b) after the arrival of the office staff at 8.20a.m.

   c) during the directors daily meeting with Heads of departments (9.00a.m.–9.20a.m.)

6. The mean height of 2000 children in a college is 65 cm. with a standard deviation of 3.5 cm. Assuming the heights to be Normally distributed, find how many students are of:

   a) height 72 cm., and over

   b) height less than 60 cm.

   c) between 64 cm. and 68 cm.

   Determine the upper and lower quartile heights.

7. It is known that the heights of certain plants are Normally distributed and that 8.9% of the plants are under 35 cm and 4.9% are over 57 cm. If 1000 plants are selected at random, how many are expected to have heights between 44 and 50 cm?

8. i) The life of a certain type of battery (assuming continuous use) is known to be approximately Normally distributed with mean 20 hours and standard deviation 30 minutes. Calculate the probability that a randomly selected battery lasts for:

   (a) between 19 and 20.5 hours

   (b) between 19.25 and 19.75 hours

   (c) More than 19.5 hours

   (d) Less than 19 hours 17.5 minutes.

   If 6.3% of the batteries last less than 'K' hours, find the value of K.

   ii) If the batteries are checked immediately after manufacture, and the faulty ones are discarded, find the probability that a batch of 20 newly manufactured batteries contains at least 2 faulty ones, if it is known that 6% of the batteries manufactured are faulty.

   State any assumptions that you make.

9. A company that manufactures batteries guarantees them for a life of 24 months.

   i) If the average life has been found to be 33 months, with a standard deviation of 4 months, what proportion of batteries would be expected to have to be replaced under guarantee if a Normal distribution is assumed for battery lifetimes?

   ii) If the company's annual sales are 10,000 at a profit of £5 each, and each replacement costs the company £12, find the net profit.

   iii) The company is considering extending the guarantee to 27 months, and estimates that this extra offer will increase sales to 12,000 per annum.

   Consider whether or not this change in policy would be to the company's advantage.

10. A manufacturer of electrical light bulbs finds that the output has a length of life that is approximately Normally distributed with mean 856 hours and standard deviation of 127 hours.

    a) Find the percentage of light bulbs which can be expected to have a life between 720 and 950 hours.

    b) If the manufacturer guarantees a minimal life of 700 hours and will replace, free of charge, any bulbs that fail under guarantee, find the percentage of bulbs the manufacturer can expect to replace.

    c) If the manufacturer is now prepared to replace 5% of all bulbs produced, what figure could he set as the minimal life expectancy on the guarantee?

11. An aptitude test, which is marked out of 100, is widely used in colleges. From past experience it is known that the distribution of marks in Normal and that the average mark is 56 with a standard deviation of 6.

    If, in a particular college, 250 students take the test, calculate

    a) the percentage of students expected to obtain more than 47 marks.

    b) the expected number of students obtaining more than 70 marks.

    c) the mark below which 33% of the students are expected to score.

12. a) A television company finds that the average time spent repairing a television set is 2.2 hours with a standard deviation of 0.5 hours. The actual time is found to be approximately Normally distributed. The cost to the company for repairs is £8 per hour.

    i) What is the maximum cost for 95% of the repairs?

    ii) What proportion of the repairs costs less than £16?

    b) A minimum charge of £15 is made with up to one hour's work included. For repairs requiring between one and two hours, an additional charge of £4 is made and similarly £4 is added for repairs requiring between two and three hours. For any additional time spent, a further £2 is added.

    Would you expect the firm to make a profit with this pricing structure?

13. An automatic machine filling jars with jam does so with a Normal distribution of the net weights. The standard deviation of this process is 3 grams.

    a) If the machine is set to fill the jars with a mean net weight of 345 grams of jam, what percentage of jars are expected to have a net weight of more than 340 grams?

    b) To what mean net weight should the machine be set if only 0.1% of the jars may have a net weight of jam less than 340 grams and, if the factory cost of jam is 12 pence per 340 grams, what is the mean cost of filling a jar with jam?

Short Answers

1. a) 0.1587
    b) 0.0192
    c) 0.0594
    d) 0.9332
    e) 0.5
    f) 0.8185
    g) 0.0403
    h) 0.1693

2. a) 2.17
    b) 1.93
    c) 0.92
    d) −2.51

3. a) 0.0808
    b) 0.6554
    c) 0.1587
    d) 0.3848
    e) 0.0792
    f) 0.8041

4. a) 3085
    b) 668
    c) 6915
    d) 8413

5. a) 6
    b) 210
    c) 34

6. a) 46
    b) 153
    c) 831
    62.65, 67.35

7. 0.2946

8. i) a) 0.8185
        b) 0.2417
        c) 0.8413
        d) 0.0401
        K = 19.235
    ii) 0.3395

9. i)   0.0122
    ii)   £48,536
    iii) £50,380

10. a) 0.6281
    b) 0.1093
    c) 647.085

11. a) 93.32%
    b) 2.45
    c) 53.36

12. a) i)   £24.18
        ii) 0.3446
    b) Yes (£4.10 Profit)

13. a) 95.25%
    b) 12.33 pence

13 | Correlation and Regression

1. Introduction

In earlier chapters our study of statistics has been confined to problems and procedures involving a single variable, but there are numerous business applications of statistics that involve a study of two or more variables. In this chapter we consider the relationship between two variables and, in particular, introduce the topics of correlation and regression. These topics can be developed to consider more than two variables but this is beyond the scope of this text, which forms the basis for a more advanced study.

2. Correlation

Correlation analysis enables us to study and measure the relationship between two variables. Such a relationship may be linear (ie following a straight line relationship) or may be non–linear, but we will confine our study to linear correlation.

The relationship between two variables can be examined visually by means of a scatter diagram.

2.1 Scatter Diagrams

A scatter diagram can be drawn to examine the possible relationship between two variables. An observed real–life situation, where we have a series of paired observations, can be represented on a scatter diagram by plotting the observed points on coordinate axes in a similar way to drawing a graph but without joining up the points. Such diagrams may reveal a pattern suggesting a relationship between the two variables.

Examples of different types of scatter diagrams which might be observed in real–life situations are given below. In each case a line or curve is superimposed on to the scatter diagram indicating a possible relationship between the two variables.

Diagram 13.1

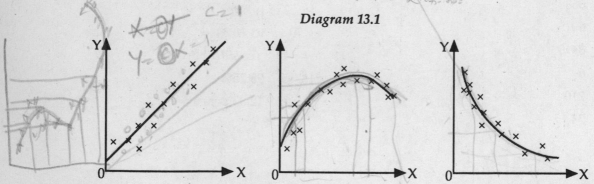

The drawing of scatter diagrams will be considered further in section 3.1.

2.2 The Correlation Coefficient

The linear relationship between two variables can be measured by calculating the Correlation Coefficient – usually denoted by the letter r, where

$$r = \frac{\sum XY - n\bar{X}\bar{Y}}{\sqrt{(\sum X^2 - n\bar{X}^2)(\sum Y^2 - n\bar{Y}^2)}}$$

The correlation coefficient, r, will always take a value in the range −1 to +1. If the value of r is positive, we have 'positive correlation' indicating that as one variable increases, the other also increases. If the value of r is negative, we have 'negative correlation' indicating that as one variable increases, the other decreases.

If r = +1, it indicates perfect positive correlation (ie the points lie exactly on a straight line with a positive gradient). If r = −1, it indicates perfect negative correlation (ie the points lie exactly on a straight line with a negative gradient).

Generally, the closer the absolute value of r is to 1, the stronger the correlation between the two variables (ie the stronger the linear relationship).

The figures in Diagram 13.2 provide an indication of the possible types of scatter, and the associated values of r, when a linear relationship between two variables is assumed.

Diagram 13.2

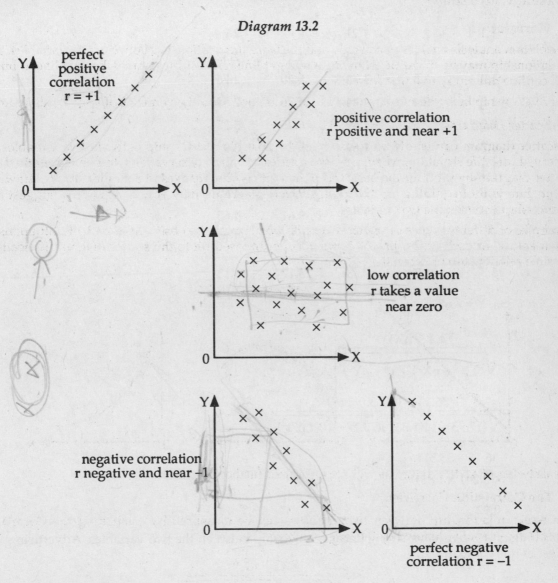

133

It should be noted that calculation of the correlation coefficient is a strictly mathematical method. It is thus up to the user to decide whether or not it is reasonable to suggest a linear relationship between the two variables in question in the first place.

Example

The following data refers to a company's advertising expenditure and corresponding sales figures over a period of ten successive months.

Advertising (£'000):	1.1	1.2	1.2	1.2	1.3	1.3	1.4	1.5	1.5	1.6
Sales (£'000):	2.0	2.1	2.3	2.4	2.5	3.0	3.0	3.1	3.1	3.2

Calculate the correlation coefficient and interpret it.

X	Y	X^2	Y^2	XY
1.1	2	1.21	4	2.2
1.2	2.1	1.44	4.41	2.52
1.2	2.3	1.44	5.29	2.76
1.2	2.4	1.44	5.76	2.88
1.3	2.5	1.69	6.25	3.25
1.3	3	1.69	9	3.9
1.4	3	1.96	9	4.2
1.5	3.1	2.25	9.61	4.65
1.5	3.1	2.25	9.61	4.65
1.6	3.2	2.56	10.24	5.12
13.3	26.7	17.93	73.17	36.13

$\bar{X} = 1.33$; $\bar{Y} = 2.67$

$$r = \frac{\Sigma XY - n\bar{X}\bar{Y}}{\sqrt{(\Sigma X^2 - n\bar{X}^2)(\Sigma Y^2 - n\bar{Y}^2)}}$$

$$= \frac{36.13 - 10(1.33)(2.67)}{\sqrt{(17.93 - 10(1.33)^2)(73.17 - 10(2.67)^2)}}$$

$$= \frac{36.13 - 35.511}{\sqrt{0.241 \times 1.881}}$$

$$= 0.92$$

This value of r suggests a strong linear relationship between the two variables 'Advertising' and 'Sales' in this company.

3. Regression Analysis

Regression analysis is concerned with the study of functional relationships between two or more variables. It provides us with a technique that enables us to estimate a functional relationship involving a number of variables though exact functional relationships are unlikely to reflect real–life situations.

Functional relationships may take a variety of forms but we will confine our study to the simplest type – a linear relationship.

Example

Consider the following situation:

Cylinders are loaded onto lorries at a loading ramp. From past experience it is known that it takes 4 minutes to prepare the site before loading can begin and that it takes 3 minutes per cylinder for loading.

From this information we know:

If 10 cylinders are loaded it will take $4 + 10 \times 3$ minutes.

If 20 cylinders are loaded it will take $4 + 20 \times 3$ minutes etc.

To express this relationship in mathematical form we may denote by Y the time taken to load (in minutes), and by X the number of cylinders in the load. We may then set up the following equation:

$Y = 4 + 3X$ (loading time equation)

This is a strict functional relationship between the variables X and Y, with the loading time (Y) depending upon the number of cylinders to be loaded (X). By substituting for X we can use the expression to predict the time taken to load a given number of cylinders.

For example, to find the time taken to load 30 cylinders, we can substitute $X = 30$ into the equation to find Y.

We then have

$Y = 4 + 3(30) = \textbf{94 minutes}$

We can refer to the variable Y as the dependent variable and the variable X as the independent variable.

In a real–life situation we would find that our predictions would not be exact and the time would vary, even for the same load size, due to factors outside of our control. In the next section we will consider such a situation.

3.1 Scatter Diagram of an Observed Situation

An observed real–life situation, such as the 'loading ramp' referred to in the example above, can be represented on a scatter diagram as indicated in section 2.1. A Scatter Diagram is drawn with the dependent variable on the vertical axis and the independent variable on the horizontal axis. Such a diagram may reveal a pattern suggesting a relationship between the two variables.

Example

Let us again consider the above example of the loading ramp. If the real–life situation were actually observed, then the results could be similar to those illustrated on the scatter diagram below.

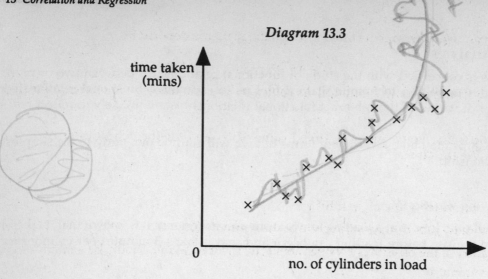

Diagram 13.3

We can immediately see that there is no indication of an exact relationship, as we would expect in a real–life situation, but the scatter of points is sufficiently distinct to suggest that there may be a 'linear' relationship between the two variables. In Section 2.2 we considered how to measure this linear relationship.

The next question is how to estimate this linear relationship.

3.2 Linear Regression

As indicated in section 3.1, a scatter diagram of an observed situation may reveal a possible linear relationship between two variables. Linear regression is concerned with estimating this linear relationship.

In general terms, a linear relationship will take the form:

$$Y = a + bX$$

and the problem consists of calculating values for a and b from the set of pairs of observed values for X and Y.

The method most frequently employed for obtaining the line of 'best fit' is called the 'method of least squares' which we will now consider with reference to the diagram below.

Diagram 13.4

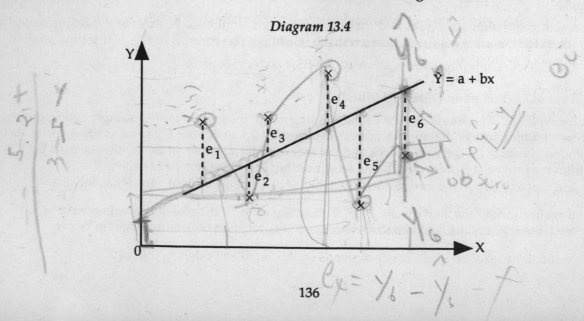

136

The proposed regression equation to be fitted through the scatter is denoted by

$$\hat{Y} = a + bX$$

where $\hat{Y}$ is used to distinguish the theoretical Y values on this line from the observed Y values. $\hat{Y}$ is read as y 'hat'.

e_i represents the difference between the observed value of Y_i and the theoretical value of Y_i on the regression line. We thus have

$$e_i = Y_i - \hat{Y}_i$$

The Least Squares criteria for a line of 'best fit' are:

i) The line should pass through the centre of the scatter ie $\Sigma e_i = 0$

ii) The variation of the observed Y values about the theoretical line should be a minimum ie Σe_i^2 is a minimum

Using mathematical methods that are not considered here, it can be shown that when fitting a straight line, these requirements are met if the estimates for a and b are calculated as follows:

$$b = \frac{\Sigma(X - \bar{X})(Y - \bar{Y})}{\Sigma(X - \bar{X})^2} = \frac{\Sigma XY - n\bar{X}\bar{Y}}{\Sigma X^2 - n\bar{X}^2} \qquad a = \bar{Y} - b\bar{X}$$

where $\bar{X}$ is the average of all the X values of the observed points

$\bar{Y}$ is the average of all the Y values

n is the number of observed points.

b can be interpreted as the gradient of the regression line, and

a can be interpreted as the point where the regression line cuts the y–axis.

Example

The following series of observations were made at a factory during the loading of cylinders on to lorries.

Time taken to load (mins):	8	9	11	12	18	19	20	24	29	30
No. of cylinders in load:	4	11	19	14	22	32	16	29	34	39

i) Plot this data on a scatter diagram and calculate the correlation coefficient.

ii) Obtain the linear regression equation that best fits the data.

iii) Use the regression equation to estimate the time taken to load:

a) 10 cylinders

b) 50 cylinders

Comment on these estimates.

Solution

i) We first identify X, the independent variable, and Y, the dependent variable as follows:

X: No. of cylinders in load

Y: Time taken to load the cylinders (mins)

as the 'time taken to load' clearly depends on the 'no. of cylinders in the load'.

Diagram 13.5

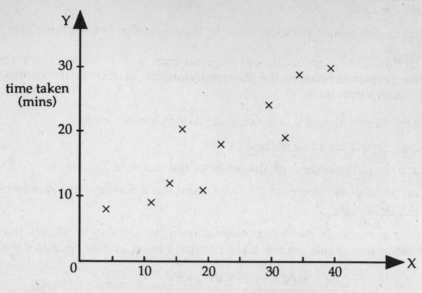

no. of cylinders in load

X	Y	XY	X^2	Y^2
4	8	16	32	64
11	9	121	99	81
19	11	361	209	121
14	12	196	168	144
22	18	484	396	324
32	19	1024	608	361
16	20	256	320	400
29	24	841	696	576
34	29	1156	986	841
39	30	1521	1170	900
220	180	5976	4684	3812

we have:

$\Sigma X = 220$ $\Sigma Y = 180$ $\Sigma X^2 = 5976$ $\Sigma XY = 4684$ $\Sigma Y^2 = 3812$

$n = 10$ $\bar{X} = 22$ $\bar{Y} = 18$

$$r = \frac{\Sigma XY - n\bar{X}\bar{Y}}{\sqrt{(\Sigma X^2 - n\bar{X}^2)(\Sigma Y^2 - n\bar{Y}^2)}}$$

$$r = \frac{4864 - 10(22)(18)}{\sqrt{(5976 - 10(22)^2)(3812 - 10(18)^2)}}$$

138

$$r = \frac{4864 - 3960}{\sqrt{(1136 \times 572)}} = \frac{724}{806.1}$$

$$r = 0.90$$

This value of the Correlation Coefficient suggests quite a good linear relationship between the two variables in question, and hence the regression line may be used to provide a reasonable estimate of 'Time taken to Load'.

ii) To estimate the Regression Line, we must calculate values for b and a.

$$b = \frac{\sum XY - n\bar{X}\bar{Y}}{\sum X^2 - n\bar{X}^2} = \frac{4684 - 10(22)(18)}{5976 - 10(22)^2}$$

$$b = \frac{4684 - 3960}{5976 - 4840} = \frac{724}{1136}$$

$$b = 0.637$$

$$a = \bar{Y} - b\bar{X}$$

$$a = 18 - 0.637(22)$$

$$a = 14$$

The regression equation is therefore

$$Y = 14 + 0.64X$$

iii) When $X = 10$, $Y = 14 + 0.64(10) = 10.4$ (minutes)

When $X = 50$, $Y = 14 + 0.64(50) = 36$ (minutes)

The estimate of 'Time' for ten cylinders can be considered as reasonably good as the correlation coefficient suggests a fairly good linear relationship between the variables. However, the estimate of 'Time' for fifty cylinders is an example of the misuse of the regression line. In the original set of data, the number of cylinders varied between 4 and 39 and while it is acceptable to assume a reasonable linear relationship within this range (and possibly a little outside it) we cannot assume that this linear relationship holds for all values of x.

Example

The following data represents a company's annual sales for one of its products over an eight year period.

YEAR	SALES (£'000)
1983	10
1984	11
1985	9
1986	12
1987	14
1988	13
1989	16
1990	15

i) Plot this data on a scatter diagram

ii) Calculate the correlation coefficient and interpret it

iii) Obtain the linear regression equation that best fits the data.

This type of example, in which the independent variable is time, can be referred to as a time series. In this type of example it is necessary to allocate values to the independent variable and a common approach is to number the years successively and allocate a value of zero to the middle year (or one of the middle years if the number of years is even). This is illustrated below:

i)

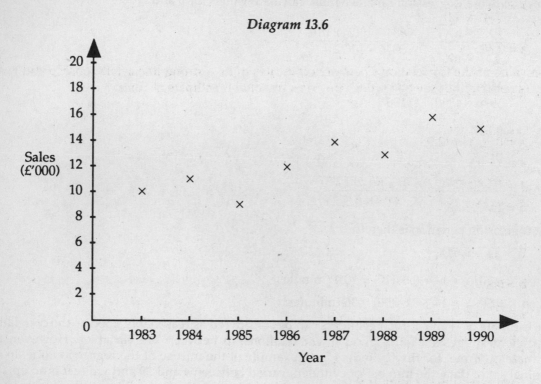

Diagram 13.6

ii)

X	Y	XY	X^2	Y^2
–3	10	–30	9	100
–2	11	–22	4	121
–1	9	–9	1	81
0	12	0	0	144
1	14	14	1	196
2	13	26	4	169
3	16	48	9	256
4	15	60	16	225
4	100	87	44	1292

$$r = \frac{\Sigma XY - n\bar{X}\bar{Y}}{\sqrt{(\Sigma X^2 - n\bar{X}^2)(\Sigma Y^2 - n\bar{Y}^2)}}$$

$$r = \frac{87 - 8(0.5)(12.5)}{\sqrt{(44 - 8(0.5)^2)(1292 - 8(12.5)^2)}}$$

$$r = \frac{87 - 50}{\sqrt{(42 \times 42)}} = \frac{37}{42}$$

r = 0.88

This value of the Correlation Coefficient indicates quite a strong linear relationship and hence the regression line may be used to provide a reasonable estimate of Sales.

iii)

$$\bar{X} = 0.5; \ \bar{Y} = 12.5$$

$$b = \frac{\Sigma XY - n\bar{X}\bar{Y}}{\Sigma X^2 - n\bar{X}^2} = \frac{87 - 8(0.5)(12.5)}{44 - 8(0.5)^2}$$

$$b = \frac{87 - 50}{44 - 2} = \frac{37}{42}$$

b = 0.88

$$a = \bar{Y} - b\bar{X}$$

$$a = 12.5 - 0.88(0.5)$$

a = 12.06

The regression equation is thus

Y = 12 + 0.88X

Exercises (Answers on page 145)

1. Draw a Scatter Diagram and then calculate the Correlation Coefficient and the Least Squares Regression Line for the following set of data

   X: 8 4 6 12 14 16 10 20 26 28
   Y: 6 2 5 10 4 10 2 14 12 16

2. In the study of computer programming, a large number of students are given instructional material and allowed to proceed at their own pace, handing in required assignments as they are completed. At the end of the course, 10 students are selected at random and given an achievement test. The results are as follows.

Hours Spent Studying:	5	10	11	20	24	25	28	32	40	45
Test Score (Max. 40):	13	8	18	25	22	25	25	24	35	35

a) Draw a scatter diagram to graphically represent this data

b) Calculate the Correlation Coefficient

c) Find the Regression Line

d) Estimate the test score for a student who studied:

   i) 15 hours

   ii) 30 hours

Comment on these estimates

3.   A firm's sales over the past nine years are given in the table below:

Year	Sales (£'000)
1982	15
1983	17
1984	19.5
1985	18
1986	22
1987	22.5
1988	26.5
1989	27.5
1990	28

a) Construct a scatter diagram of the data and comment on the functional relationship between Time and Sales as suggested by the diagram.

b) Estimate the appropriate regression equation and superimpose this on the scatter diagram

c) Estimate the expected sales in 1991

d) Given that the correlation coefficient for the above data is 0.97, interpret its meaning.

4. A Managing Director believes that there is a relationship between the age (in months) of the machines in the machine shop and the daily production of a certain component.

He asks the Production Manager to investigate, and the following data relating to twelve machines was collected.

Machine	Production per day	Age (in months)
1	151	102
2	160	99
3	95	108
4	195	95
5	270	87
6	288	84
7	190	84
8	305	82
9	228	90
10	260	86
11	218	94
12	165	100

a) Draw a scatter diagram of the data.

b) Calculate the correlation coefficient using the data from as many machines as you consider necessary. Justify the number of machines you use.

c) Find the least squares regression line and plot this line on your scatter diagram.

d) Do you agree with the Managing Director's belief? Explain.

5. An organisation's personnel department conducts an investigation into the possible correlation between 'days lost per month due to staff sickness' and 'production per month' in the previous year. The following data was collected:

Month	Days lost due to sickness	Production (in units of 1000)
Jan	22	10
Feb	28	8
Mar	18	12
Apr	16	14
May	10	17
Jun	10	18
Jul	8	20
Aug	9	19
Sep	14	15
Oct	15	16
Nov	18	13
Dec	20	11

a) Draw a scatter diagram to graphically represent this data

b) Calculate the Correlation Coefficient

c) Find the equation of Regression Line and superimpose it on the scatter diagram

d) Interpret your results

6. The Managing Director of a chain of retailing organisations believes that there is a positive relationship between sales per store and the number of employees per store in the year just past. He decides to associate 1990 sales with the number of employees per store in the 15 cities where his company has branches. The data is given below:

1990 sales (£' 000)	Number of Employees
20	150
21	250
20	170
23	230
27	270
22	230
25	250
22	160
21	180
16	110
18	120
23	220
22	230
20	180
15	100

a) Construct a scatter diagram

b) Estimate the regression coefficients and discuss their meaning.

c) Draw the regression line on the scatter diagram

d) Comment on the 'fit' of the regression line given that the correlation coefficient is approximately 0.89.

Short Answers

1. $Y = 0.505 + 0.527X$

    $r = 0.86$

2. $Y = 8.489 + 0.6046X$

    $r = 0.92$

    $X = 15, Y = 17.56$

    $X = 30, Y = 26.63$

3. Assuming 1982 corresponds to $x = -4$, 1983 to $x = -3$, etc

    $Y = 21.778 + 1.7X$

    $r = 0.975$

    $X = 5, Y = 30.28$

4. $Y = 837.543 - 6.774X$

    $r = 0.9$

5. $Y = 24.045 - 0.6146X$

    $r = 0.978$

6. $Y = -138.897 + 15.662X$

    $r = 0.89$

BUSINESS MATHEMATICS AND STATISTICS
2nd Edition
A Francis

This book provides a thorough grounding in basic mathematical and statistical techniques to students of business and professional studies. There are many self-testing exercises and fully worked examination questions.

> **COURSES ON WHICH THIS BOOK IS KNOWN TO BE USED:**
> Accountancy Foundation courses; BTEC Business and Finance; ACCA; CIMA; ICSA; CII; AAT
> *On reading list of CIMA*

CONTENTS:

Data and their Presentation • Sampling and Data Collection • Data and their Accuracy • Frequency Distributions and Charts • General Charts and Graphs • Statistical Measures • The Arithmetic Mean • The Median • The Mode and Other Measures of Location • Measures of Dispersion and Skewness • The Standard Deviation • Quantiles and the Quartile Deviation • Regression and Correlation • Linear Functions and Graphs • Regression Techniques • Correlation Techniques • Time Series Analysis • Time Series Model • Time Series Trend • Seasonal Variation and Forecasting • Index Numbers • Index Relatives • Composite Index Numbers • Special Published Indices • Compounding, Discounting and Annuities • Interest and Depreciation • Present Value and Investment Appraisal • Annuities • Business Equations and Graphs • Functions and Graphs • Linear Equations • Quadratic and Cubic Equations • Differentiation and Integration • Costs, Revenue and Profit Functions • Probability • Set Theory and Enumeration • Introduction to Probability • Conditional Probability and Expectation • Further Probability • Combinations and Permutations • Binomial and Poisson Distributions • Normal Distribution • Specialised Business Applications • Linear Inequalities • Matrices • Inventory Control • Answers to Questions.

REVIEW COMMENTS:

'..it is a model of logical organisation and clear presentation.'

The Mathematical Gazette"

'This is the kind of book which business and accountancy students at undergraduate level will love — it is very detailed and thorough on the applied business side, and not too theoretical in nature.' **"IMA Journal"**

> *Also available as ELBS edition in member countries at local currency equivalent price of £2.30*

> ISBN: 1 870941 02 0
> Extent: 432 pp
> Size: 276 × 219

Free Lecturers' Supplement

QUANTITATIVE TECHNIQUES
3rd Edition
T Lucey

This book provides a sound understanding of quantitative techniques. It includes many exercises and examination questions both with and without answers.

COURSES ON WHICH THIS BOOK IS KNOWN TO BE USED:
BTEC HNC/D, ACCA, CIMA, CIPFA, ICSA, IComA, IDPM, BA Business Studies.

On reading lists of ACCA, CIMA, IDPM and IComA

CONTENTS:

Probability and Decision Making • Decision Trees • Statistics: Statistical Inference, Hypotheses Testing • Correlation and Regression • Multiple and Non-linear Regression • Forecasting and Time Series Analysis • Calculus • Inventory Control • Queueing • Simulation • Linear Programming • Transportation • Assignment • Network Analysis • Financial Mathematics • Investment Appraisal • Matrix Algebra • Replacement Analysis • Application of Computers in Quantitative Techniques • Statistical and Financial Tables • Examination Techniques • Solutions to Exercises and Examination Questions.

REVIEW COMMENTS:

'This book is written in the form of a self-study course with plenty of examples and test exercises. Solutions to the exercises are given at the end of the book. One of the best characteristics of the approach is the use of flowcharts to illustrate the procedural steps for each method, and the whole book has a clarity and a sequential development that are highly desirable in a technical workbook.'

"British Book News"

Also available as ELBS edition in member countries at local currency equivalent price of £2.50

Free Lecturers' Supplement

ISBN: 0 905435 82 6

Extent: 688 pp

Size: 276 × 219 mm

QUANTITATIVE TECHNIQUES
3rd Edition
T Lucey

This book provides a sound understanding of quantitative techniques. It includes many exercises and examination questions both with and without answers.

COURSES ON WHICH THIS BOOK IS KNOWN TO BE USED:
BTEC HNC/D, ACCA, CIMA, CIPFA, ICSA, IComA, IDPM, BA Business Studies.

On reading lists of ACCA, CIMA, IDPM and IComA

CONTENTS:

Probability and Decision Making • Decision Trees • Statistics: Statistical Inference, Hypotheses Testing • Correlation and Regression • Multiple and Non-linear Regression • Forecasting and Time Series Analysis • Calculus • Inventory Control • Queueing • Simulation • Linear Programming • Transportation • Assignment • Network Analysis • Financial Mathematics • Investment Appraisal • Matrix Algebra • Replacement Analysis • Application of Computers in Quantitative Techniques • Statistical and Financial Tables • Examination Techniques • Solutions to Exercises and Examination Questions.

REVIEW COMMENTS:

'This book is written in the form of a self-study course with plenty of examples and test exercises. Solutions to the exercises are given at the end of the book. One of the best characteristics of the approach is the use of flowcharts to illustrate the procedural steps for each method, and the whole book has a clarity and a sequential development that are highly desirable in a technical workbook.'

"British Book News"

Also available as ELBS edition in member countries at local currency equivalent price of £2.50

Free Lecturers' Supplement

ISBN: 0 905435 82 6

Extent: 688 pp

Size: 276 × 219 mm

REFRESHER IN BASIC MATHEMATICS
2nd Edition
RN Rowe

This book is aimed at those students who have difficulty with basic mathematics as well as those who wish to refresh their understanding of the subject (perhaps due to a prolonged absence from study). The text covers ten units, each of which consists of an introduction to the topic and a series of worked examples (graded by level of difficulty) followed by exercises.

The book is suitable for use on any course in further or higher education involving a quantitative component.

COURSES ON WHICH THIS BOOK IS KNOWN TO BE USED:
HNC/D Business and Finance; HNC/D Computing; BA Business Studies; BA Economics; BA Social Sciences; Diploma in Health Administration; Accountancy Foundation courses; Access Courses; MBA; DMS.

CONTENTS:

Fractions • Decimals • Percentages • Elementary Algebra • Powers • Coordinates and Graphs • The Straight Line • Simple Linear Equations • Simultaneous Equations • Quadratic Equations • Achievement Test • Tutors Section • Appendices: Calculators; Rounding.

REVIEW COMMENTS:

'Well liked by students ...' 'It is an excellent book, much appreciated by student.' 'I can't get it back from a student!' **Lecturers**

ISBN: 1 870941 61 6

Extent: 96 pp

Size: 216 × 138 mm

A First Course in
STATISTICS
D Booth

This book provides a core text for introductory level courses in statistics. It assumes the student has no prior knowledge of statistics whatsoever and no more than an ability to handle simple arithmetic.

COURSES ON WHICH THIS BOOK IS KNOWN TO BE USED:
BTEC Business and Secretarial Studies; RSA; LCCI; AAT Certificate.

CONTENTS:

This is Statistics • Fundamental Ideas • Asking the Question • Collecting the Data • Deriving the Statistics • Communicating the Results • **Asking Questions** • Questions and Statistics • Who Asks the Questions • How to Ask Questions • How Not to Ask Questions • Questionnaire Design • When to Ask Questions • **Collection of Data** • Primary Data • Probability and Sampling • Organising the Data • Tabulation of Data • Secondary Data • Graphical Representation of Data • **Deriving the Statistics** • Single Statistics • Dispersion • Multiple Statistics • Index Numbers • Regression • Correlation • Time Series • **Communicating the Results** • The General Principles of Presentation • Demonstration Tables • Pictorial Represent-ation • The Use of Words • Answers to Exercises.

REVIEW COMMENTS:

'The book is a breath of fresh air to those who think statistics is an essentially practical subject, as it has not only a section on the derivation of individual statistics but also three sections dealing with the practical details and problems associated with 'Asking the question', 'Collecting the data' and 'Communicating the results' which are so often given such little emphasis in introductory statistical texts ... Each chapter of each section ends with a short series of exercises, answers being provided only to alternate questions, a nice touch to cut out the "right answer/wrong calculation" effect yet still giving students some answers...'
"The Mathematical Gazette"

Free Lecturers' Supplement

ISBN: 0 905435 84 2
Extent: 304 pp
Size: 246 × 189 mm

A First Course in
COST AND MANAGEMENT ACCOUNTING
T Lucey

This book provides a broad introduction to cost and management accounting for those who have not studied the subject before. It is written in a clear, straightforward fashion without technical jargon or unnecessary detail. The text includes many practical examples, diagrams, exercises and examination questions. Features include several objective tests for self-assessment and assignments for activity-based learning.

COURSES ON WHICH THIS BOOK IS KNOWN TO BE USED:
BTEC National Business and Finance; RSA; LCCI; AAT; Management and Supervisory Studies; Business Studies and Marketing courses; Access courses; Purchasing and Supply and any course requiring a broad, non-specialist treatment of cost and management accounting.

CONTENTS:

Cost Analysis and Cost Ascertainment • What is Product Costing and Cost Accounting? • Elements of Cost • Labour, Materials and Overheads • Calculating Product Costs • Job, Batch and Contract Costing • Service, Process and Joint Product Costing • Information for Planning and Control • What is Planning and Control? • Cost Behaviour • Budgetary Planning • Budgetary Control • Cash Budgeting • Standard Costing • Variance Analysis • Information for Decision Making and Performance Appraisal • What is Decision Making? • Marginal Costing • Break-even Analysis • Pricing Decisions • Investment Appraisal • Performance Appraisal of Departments and Divisions.

Free Lecturers' Supplement

ISBN: 1 870941 54 3

Extent: 300 pp

Size: 246 × 189 mm

A First Course in
BUSINESS STUDIES
S Danks

NEW

This lively text provides a thorough introduction to Business Studies. Each chapter includes: a summary; review questions; practice examination questions; multiple choice/completion questions; recent examination questions; a student-centred assignment.

COURSES ON WHICH THIS BOOK IS EXPECTED TO BE USED:
RSA, PE1, LCCI, GCSE and BTEC courses.

CONTENTS:

Development of Economic Activity • Population • International Trade • Commercial Banks • The Government and Banking • Types of Business Organisations – Private Enterprise • Types of Business Organisations – Public Enterprises • Business Organisations and Management • Location and the Size of Firms • Marketing • Advertising and Sales Promotion • Markets and Middlemen • Retailing • Transport • Consumer Protection • Business Finance • Controlling Business Costs • Insurance • The Stock Exchange • Recruitment, Selection and Training • People and Work • Communication • Postal Services and Telecommunications • Industrial Relations • The Government and Business.

ISBN: 1 870941 73 X

Extent: 350 pp (Approx)

Size: 246 × 189 mm

Free Lecturers' Supplement